Household spending in Britain

What can it teach us about poverty?

Household spending in Britain

What can it teach us about poverty?

Mike Brewer, Alissa Goodman and Andrew Leicester

JOSEPH ROWNTREE
FOUNDATION

First published in Great Britain in April 2006 by

The Policy Press
Fourth Floor, Beacon House
Queen's Road
Bristol BS8 1QU
UK

Tel no   +44 (0)117 331 4054
Fax no   +44 (0)117 331 4093
Email   tpp-info@bristol.ac.uk
www.policypress.org.uk

Published for the Joseph Rowntree Foundation by The Policy Press

10-digit ISBN 1 86134 854 1
13-digit ISBN 978 1 86134 854 8

British Library Cataloguing in Publication Data
A catalogue record for this book is available from the British Library.

Library of Congress Cataloging-in-Publication Data
A catalog record for this book has been requested.

Mike Brewer is programme director of the Direct Tax and Welfare sector; **Alissa Goodman** is programme director of the Education, Employment and Evaluation sector; **Andrew Leicester** is a senior research economist in the Consumption and Savings sector, all at the Institute for Fiscal Studies.

The **Joseph Rowntree Foundation** has supported this project as part of its programme of research and innovative development projects, which it hopes will be of value to policy makers, practitioners and service users. The facts presented and views expressed in this report are, however, those of the authors and not necessarily those of the Foundation.

Cover design by Qube Design Associates, Bristol
Printed in Great Britain by Hobbs the Printers Ltd, Southampton

Contents

List of figures and tables

Figures

Tables

Acknowledgements

The authors are very grateful to Mark Hinman and Chris Goulden, project managers from the Joseph Rowntree Foundation (JRF), and to members of the advisory group: Stephen Balchin (Department for Work and Pensions, DWP), Elaine Squires (DWP), Asghar Zaidi (DWP), Caroline Lakin (Office for National Statistics, ONS), Ian Walker (University of Warwick), Peter Smith (University of Southampton), Richard Berthoud (Institute for Social and Economic Research, ISER), Paul Cann (Help the Aged), Richard Wilson (Help the Aged), Kitty Stewart (London School of Economics, Centre for Analysis of Social Exclusion, LSE/CASE) and Sally West (Age Concern). We also wish to thank Robert Chote at the Institute for Fiscal Studies (IFS), and Donald Hirsch (special adviser to the Joseph Rowntree Foundation), for comments on earlier drafts of the report. Data from the Family Expenditure Survey (FES) and Expenditure and Food Survey (EFS) are © Crown Copyright, and are used with the permission of the Controller of Her Majesty's Stationery Office (HMSO). None of the institutions mentioned here bears any responsibility for the analysis or interpretation of the data reported here: the authors alone are responsible for any errors and omissions.

Executive summary

Chapter 1

- Patterns in household expenditure have been largely overlooked in the recent policy debate about living standards and poverty. But spending probably provides a better picture of long-run financial circumstances than income, since over the life course incomes tend first to rise sharply with age, and then decline in later life, but people use borrowing and saving to make sure that their spending is more even over time.
- Both income and expenditure are subject to measurement error, but due to the way that spending is collected in UK surveys, there is good reason to think that there may be less measurement error at the very bottom of the spending distribution than at the very bottom of the income distribution, and that expenditure may therefore be a more accurate guide to very low living standards.

Chapter 2

- Some things we know about living standards are unaffected whether we consider income or spending. For example, real living standards have in general been rising both over time and across generations, and this is reflected in increases in both the average income and average spending of British households.
- Relative poverty rates rose over much of the 1980s, whether we consider income or spending. This occurred as inequality widened across both the income and spending distributions. However, the increase in spending poverty was much smaller than the increase in income poverty.
- But in more recent years, families on the lowest incomes have seen incomes rise faster, on average, than middle-income households, reducing income poverty rates.

This has not been the case for the lowest spenders, and spending poverty rates have continued to rise. As a result, the gap that developed between income and spending poverty rates in the 1980s has now disappeared.

- Poverty rates using spending have gone up since 1996/97. In the whole population, the proportion of individuals living in households with less than 60% of the median spending has risen from 20% to 22%, a rise of 12% (or 2.3 percentage points). This is exactly the same as the proportional fall in the income poverty rate, which dropped by 12% over this time. Since the Labour government came to power, the child poverty rate has risen from 25% to around 27% (a rise of 11%) using expenditure, while it fell from around 33% to 28% (a fall of around 15%) using income. Pensioner poverty has remained roughly unchanged on spending, but on income pensioner poverty has fallen rapidly.
- Who we think of as poor also differs depending on whether we use income or spending as a guide. Pensioners are poorer on their spending than their income, while self-employed and unemployed people seeking work are less likely to be poor when considering spending compared to income.

Chapter 3

- Households at the very bottom of the income distribution have disproportionately high spending. For example, the median weekly spending of the poorest 1% of the income distribution, at £192 per week (expressed as the equivalent spending for a couple with no children), was the same as the average spending observed among those a third of the way up the income distribution.

- It might be that these lowest-income households are spending more than households with higher incomes because they are only on this income for a short period of time and are drawing down savings or running up debt. Or, alternatively, because their incomes are mis-measured. In any of these cases it is likely that spending provides a better guide to living standards for these households.

- By contrast, households at the very bottom of the expenditure distribution do not appear to have incomes disproportionately high compared to their spending. This suggests that there may be less measurement error at the very bottom of the spending distribution than the very bottom of the income distribution, and that expenditure is therefore a more accurate guide to very low living standards. A more reliable picture of who is genuinely poor may therefore be obtained from an examination of the bottom of the spending distribution rather than the income distribution.

Chapter 4

- Since 1999, there has been a series of significant increases to benefits for those aged 60 or over. These have affected some pensioners more than others. For example, pensioners entitled to means-tested benefits have seen much bigger increases to their benefit entitlements than those not entitled, and pensioners aged under 80 have seen bigger increases than pensioners aged over 80.

- Pensioners who have seen the biggest increases in benefit entitlements have also seen the biggest increases in their spending over this time. This suggests that, despite being low spenders on average, pensioners are spending more, and on non-essential items, in response to increases in their benefit entitlement.

Chapter 5

- Household expenditure provides an important complement to household income for monitoring living standards and poverty. It would be a valuable addition to our knowledge of poverty in the Britain if expenditure poverty was monitored more regularly and more thoroughly, whether by government or other organisations.

- The case for assessing trends in expenditure poverty in Britain is strengthened by the fact that Britain has very good expenditure data, from the Expenditure and Food Survey (EFS). Two improvements to this data could be made. First, a useful addition to the EFS would be more information on the length of ownership and price paid for consumer durables already owned. Second, bigger sample sizes would allow for much more robust monitoring to be carried out, particularly among subgroups of the population.

- Our findings provide some lessons for the government's future child poverty targets. A recurring theme throughout our report is the strong likelihood of either measurement error or very transitory incomes at the bottom of the income scale. Our evidence suggests that reducing the income poverty rate to 'among the best in Europe' by 2020 is likely to avoid moving into territory where incomes could be mis-measured or just transitorily very low.

- Our findings suggest that the government's benefit, tax credit and other policies have been relatively successful in bringing down the number of people who are income-poor, and among pensioners have also led to increases in spending, particularly on items other than food and fuel. However, these policies have not yet led to reductions in measures of spending poverty among the population. Since expenditure poverty is more likely to reflect longer-term inequalities than income, our findings highlight the difficulties of reducing such entrenched inequalities, and suggest that other policy measures, which more fundamentally alter the underlying distribution of income, are perhaps more likely to reduce these significantly.

Introduction

Are we getting better off or are we worse off? When answering such questions about our living standards, it is usual to examine trends in income. A higher income (adjusted for changes in the cost of living) is assumed to represent an increase in overall well-being, perhaps because of the opportunities it provides and because of a wealth of evidence that higher incomes are positively correlated with, among other things, health status, life expectancy, housing conditions and so on. Furthermore, the current Labour government's high profile targets for reducing child poverty, and its policy commitments to reduce pensioner poverty, tend to focus on household income as a measure of household well-being. Government policy has also focused on supplementing incomes as its main means of improving the well-being of pensioners and families with children.

However, income is not the only measure of living standards available. One particular problem with focusing on income is that it may reflect many temporary differences between people that need not be meaningful or important in the longer term. For example, incomes tend to vary in the short term because of irregular income streams, such as self-employment income or irregular bonuses, or because of temporary periods of unemployment or sickness. Incomes also tend to vary over people's lifetimes, through trends in earnings related to age, experience or seniority, as well as through employment breaks for childrearing, retirement and so forth.

Yet living standards do not vary quite so much if people can anticipate or in other ways insure against these 'income shocks' and lifecycle trends, and smooth them out over time. This is done by making use of savings and borrowing: by saving while working and running down savings to maintain living standards when

retired; or by borrowing when earnings are low, and repaying debt when earnings are higher. It may also be achieved by transfers between household members. If spending is maintained at a more constant level even while incomes are variable, then spending will be a better proxy for lifetime, or 'permanent' income. Disparities in expenditure may therefore tell us something about permanent inequalities in welfare which income dispersion cannot[1].

Although there has been much recent emphasis on the advantages of measures of household expenditure (as a proxy for consumption) in assessing household welfare in more academic circles[2], this has yet to work its way into the mainstream poverty measurement debate in the UK: there were no measures of expenditure or consumption considered in the government's recent child poverty measurement consultation (see DWP, 2003)[3].

This report seeks to rectify this. It has three aims:

---

[1]   Spending can also vary over short periods of time for reasons unrelated to variations in living standards – for more on this, see p 4. For more information on income and expenditure as measures of well-being more generally, see, among others, Goodman and Oldfield (2004).

[2]   For example, see Blundell and Preston (1998), Slesnick (1993) and Meyer and Sullivan (2003, 2004).

[3]   The new measure of child poverty, to be used to track progress to the 2010 target, includes measures of material deprivation, based on the ability to afford particular goods and services (DWP, 2003). However, these deprivation measures differ fundamentally from measures of total expenditure, since they focus on the ownership of specific items rather than total expenditure on all items.

- To show what trends in household expenditure can tell us about the changing incidence of poverty in Britain, compared with measures based on income alone (see Chapter 2). This will add to a literature considering a wide range of other ways, besides measuring low income, of looking at poverty. For example the New Policy Institute's annual report considers low pay, education, health, material deprivation, crime and housing, but does not consider trends in household spending (see Palmer et al, 2004). Hills and Stewart (2005) also provide a comprehensive summary of many aspects of poverty in Britain. Their work touches on spending as an indicator of well-being in the context of child poverty.
- To investigate the robustness of using household income for measuring poverty by examining spending levels among the households with the very lowest incomes (see Chapter 3). This is also helpful for assessing the feasibility of achieving the government's ambitious poverty reduction targets based on income-based definitions of poverty.
- To examine recent changes in spending among low-income pensioners to give us a clearer idea of the impact of the recent very large increases in means-tested benefits (see Chapter 4). Pensioners are to be found lower down the expenditure distribution than the income distribution, but it is not known how their expenditure has reacted to the relatively large increases in means-tested benefits they have experienced since 1999, a policy which was clearly designed to improve the well-being of some of the poorest in our society. Our focus will be on pensioners, since other similar work has addressed this issue for families with children, the other group seeing large increases in means-tested benefits since 1997 (see Gregg et al, 2005, in Hills and Stewart, 2005).

Our conclusions, and recommendations for policy and research are outlined in Chapter 5; much of the technical detail is contained in the Appendix. The rest of this chapter presents the theoretical reasons for using household spending as a guide to poverty, and describes the data sources used in the rest of the report.

Using the expenditure of households to measure poverty

There is no single financial indicator of well-being that will always accurately measure people's living standards. Income may be preferred as its level can be directly affected by government policy, and because there is an argument that individuals derive welfare from income saved as well as income spent. As mentioned above, however, one problem with focusing on income is that it varies over time, whether due to relatively unpredictable short-term shocks, such as periods of unemployment or sickness or annual bonuses, and through relatively predictable longer-term trends, such as earnings rising with experience or seniority, and adults taking breaks from employment through caring responsibilities or retirement. Yet living standards do not vary as much as income if people can anticipate these changes or insure against them in some way. For example, students tend to borrow against their future earnings in order to achieve a certain standard of living while studying. Similarly, living standards might drop by far less than income when people retire because most people accumulate assets when working, and use them to maintain their quality of life once retired. Whatever mechanism is used (for example, running up or down savings or debt), the key point is that if spending is maintained at a more constant level over time even while incomes are fairly volatile, it may be that spending is a better representation of an individual's average (or 'permanent', in the economics literature) income. If so, then disparities in expenditure tell us something about permanent inequalities in living standards and well-being that variation in income cannot.

Whether people do smooth their consumption in this way is something on which there is a large academic literature. Some graphical evidence is presented below (see Figure 1.1), which shows how average income and spending vary with age, for different cohorts (a cohort refers to people born in a given decade). For each cohort, we show the median expenditure or income at each age. Note that the oldest cohorts are to the right-hand side of each figure and the youngest cohorts are to the left-hand side, showing that average living

Figure 1.1: Lifecycle income dynamics by cohort

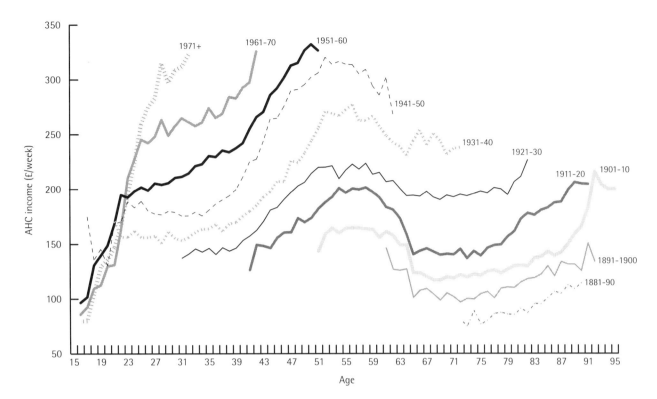

Notes: AHC: after housing costs. Shows median AHC income by 10-year birth cohort and age. Cohorts are defined in 10-year intervals according to the date of birth of the head of the household, while age is also that of the head of the household. Incomes are equivalised. Cells with fewer than 50 observations are not included in the analysis.

Source: Authors' calculations based on Family Expenditure Survey (FES) and Family Resources Survey (FRS)

standards have improved over time whether we use income or spending as the basis for measuring them.

There is a distinct lifecycle pattern in the income profiles: rapid growth in the early part of the working life, followed by a period of gentler growth during the childrearing period, and more rapid growth to a peak, after which income declines as people retire. Among pensioners, incomes are fairly stable, rising slightly at the end, probably reflecting that those living to ages of 80 or more tend to be richer than those who die before this point.

For expenditure, the lifecycle pattern appears similar, although, as we would expect, the profiles are slightly flatter, particularly for the older cohorts. Even if one is not prepared to believe that individuals fully smooth their expenditure over time in the face of uncertain or changing income streams, because of lack of access to credit markets or inability to build up a sufficient stock of savings, this flatness suggests some degree of income smoothing over the lifetime. This supports our contention that spending may give a better picture of

long-run, or 'permanent', income than income measured at one point.

A second and rather different reason for preferring expenditure to income as a measure of well-being relates to the way that estimates of the distribution of income and expenditure are produced: through large-scale surveys of private households. Given the way that these surveys are designed, it may be that expenditure is subject to less measurement error than income, especially among individuals who rely on irregular sources of informal income such as borrowing from family, or from individuals whose income is hard to record, such as self-employed people.

Of course, expenditure-based measures of poverty are not free from either measurement error or variability issues. Most spending in the UK data is recorded in a two-week diary of purchases and through interviews asking about spending on durable and expensive items over the past few months. People may accidentally or deliberately mis-record their spending. We know, for example, that the Family Expenditure Survey (FES), the main source for

Figure 1.2: Lifecycle expenditure dynamics by cohort

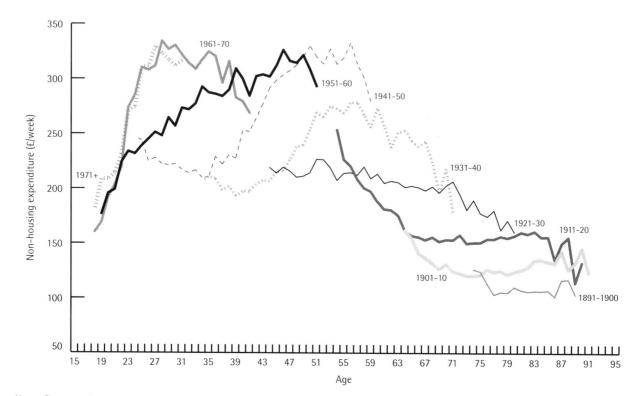

Notes: Shows median non-housing expenditure by 10-year birth cohort and age. Cohorts are defined in 10-year intervals according to the date of birth of the head of the household, while age is also that of the head of the household. Expenditure is equivalised. Cells with fewer than 50 observations are not included in the analysis.
Source: Authors' calculations based on FES

information on households' spending in the UK, under-records spending on tobacco and alcohol (see Blow et al, 2004).

Expenditure can also be variable over short periods of time because it is *lumpy*: people may spend money in one period on, say, durable goods and frozen foods, and then relatively little in the next as they live off this earlier spending. In other words, expenditure is not the same as *consumption* – people get benefits from durables such as housing, cars and televisions over a long period of time but may spend a lot of money up-front to buy these items, and then have no spending on them thereafter. Thus it is still possible to have low measured spending in any one period but to have a high standard of living[4].

So while neither income or spending are without problems as measures of living standards, spending will provide at the very least an important alternative to income as a measure of welfare, and the balance of these arguments suggests that, on average, it should better reflect longer-term differences in living standards than income[5].

Our definitions of income and expenditure and the sources of data we use are as follows:

• *Expenditure* data is taken from the FES and its successor, the Expenditure and Food Survey (EFS), between 1974 and 2002/03. Expenditure in these surveys is mostly recorded by means of a two-week diary, but also includes information on larger items such as furniture and utility bills collected through retrospective recall questions over a

---

4   Note that the expenditure data tries to address the lumpiness issue by asking people to recall spending on durable or expensive items like cars and holidays over the last six months and then taking a weekly average. However, we might be worried about the accuracy of people's recall, and whether people who spent money on a holiday before the recall period include it anyway – this would make expenditures seem too high. This is known as 'telescoping'.

---

5   A different sort of reason why policy makers might prefer using income to spending measures of poverty is that incomes are more directly responsive to government tax and benefit changes than spending. This means that the effects of given policy changes on household incomes will be more immediate, and easier to predict.

number of months which is then converted to a weekly average. We measure weekly household spending, but in general we do not include expenditure on housing (rent, mortgage payments, water payments, council tax and so on) in our measure of spending. This is because housing is particularly difficult to measure well since people with zero expenditures (who own outright, for example) will appear poorer but will still obtain consumption benefits (see Chapter 2, Box 2.1). As far as we can tell, the fact that the source for expenditure data changed between 2000/01 and 2001/02 is not relevant to understanding the recent trends in expenditure.

- *Income* data will be taken from two different sources. When we report trends in living standards and poverty over time (Chapters 2 and 3), we will focus on income from the Households Below Average Income (HBAI) series, produced by the Department for Work and Pensions (see DWP, 2005), and extended back in time by the Institute for Fiscal Studies (IFS). The income data comes from two sources – the FES between 1961 and 1993, and the Family Resources Survey (FRS) thereafter. It is defined as net household income from all sources – employment, investments, benefits and so on. We will focus on the measure of income measured *after* housing costs (rent, mortgage interest payments, housing insurance) have been deducted since our expenditure data will typically exclude housing (see above).

- When we consider how incomes and spending compare for the same households (in Chapters 4 and 5) we will need to use the same data source for both, and we therefore use a consistent income series derived from the FES and EFS between 1974 and 2002/03. The definition of income used (based on derived 'product code' variables provided within the FES/EFS) is slightly different to the income definition used in the HBAI series. However, it is also a measure of net household income from all sources, after housing costs have been deducted[6].

All our data is weighted to be nationally representative for Britain, and equivalised using the McClements scale. This allows us to compare the income and spending of households with different compositions of adults to children to a baseline household made up of a couple with no children[7]. All income and spending values are expressed in real terms (in 2002/03 prices).

---

6   Details of how the product code measure of income differs from HBAI measures and how the choice of income measure affects measured poverty are available from the authors.

7   For more on equivalence scales see, for example, Chapter 1 of Goodman et al (1997).

2

Income and expenditure poverty compared

The aim of this chapter is to show what trends in household expenditure can tell us about the changing incidence of poverty in Britain, compared with measures based on income alone. The analysis is largely descriptive, although we tentatively present some explanations for the differences in the conclusions to the report (see Chapter 5).

The first section of this chapter compares trends in average income and expenditure, and gives some summary measures of changes in the distribution of income and expenditure. The next section examines the difference in trends in the number of people who are considered poor, and the difference in the composition of the poor. Following the government's child poverty targets and its convention for measuring relative low incomes in its annual audit of poverty, *Opportunity for All*, in this second section we focus on income and spending poverty rates defined relative to the contemporary median.

As explained in Chapter 1, our measure of income is that used in the DWP's HBAI series (see DWP, 2005). HBAI income data comes from two sources – the FES between 1961 and 1993, and the FRS thereafter. It is defined as net household income from all sources – employment, investments, benefits and so on – and we focus on the measure of income measured after housing costs (rent, mortgage interest payments, housing insurance) have been deducted. Expenditure data is taken from the FES and its successor, the EFS, between 1974 and 2002/03. We do not include expenditure on housing (rent, mortgage payments, water payments, council tax etc) in our measure of spending.

Changes in the distribution of income and expenditure

The general increase in living standards over time can be seen when we consider what has happened to average incomes and spending across the whole population. Figure 2.1 shows the evolution of real mean and median HBAI income after housing costs (AHC) and non-housing expenditure. The small crosses around each line show 95% confidence intervals, reflecting sampling uncertainty.

Several points emerge from Figure 2.1. First, median values for both income and spending are well below the means, because the distribution of both income and spending are skewed, with the bulk of the population having income and spending below the mean, and both distributions having a long upper tail. Second, the time series patterns of each are similar: both show a cyclical pattern around an upward trend. Interestingly, in the early 2000s, income growth continued to be strong while expenditure growth appears to have slowed.

Figure 2.2(a) shows how income and spending at different points in the distribution changed between 1979 and 1990[1]. In each year, we divide the population up into 100 equally sized

---

[1] The average annual change in income by percentile has been shown before: see Brewer et al (2004, 2005), for example, but this is the first time such analysis has been done for expenditure. The start and end dates correspond to dates when there was a change in the Prime Minister in the UK, although such dates mean that the different periods will correspond to different parts of the economic cycle. Note that we exclude the period 1990-97 from these results; over this period income and spending grew at very similar and very low rates across the whole distribution. Figures are available on request from the authors.

Figure 2.1: Mean and median real income and expenditure (1961–2002/03)

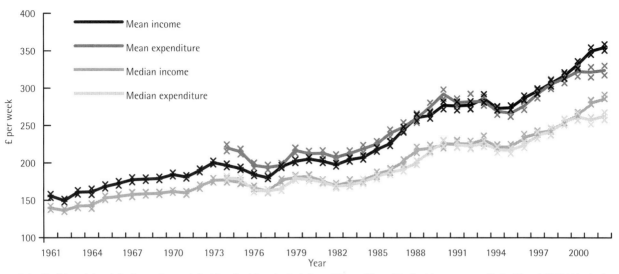

Notes: Confidence intervals for the median are derived from bootstrapping techniques; 200 repetitions of the bootstrap were run with the 6th and 195th highest values of the median giving the 95% interval.

Source: Income data from FES, 1961-92 and FRS thereafter. Expenditure data from FES, 1974-2000/01 and EFS thereafter.

groups, from poorest to richest (or lowest to highest spenders), with each group representing one 'percentile' of the population.

It is well known that income inequality grew substantially during the 1980s. Figure 2.2(a) shows that this was because the annual average growth in real incomes rises as we move up the percentiles from poor to rich. The same is true for expenditure, although the increase in expenditure inequality was smaller than the increase in income inequality: the slope of the line in Figure 2.2(a) for expenditure growth is less steep than that for income growth.

Since the period of time during which the Labour government has been in power is of particular interest to us when considering recent trends in poverty, Figure 2.2(b) shows the same analysis for income and spending growth between 1996/97 and 2002/03. For income, the fastest growth since 1996/97 has been at the very top of the distribution (the 99th percentile, roughly the richest 550,000 individuals in Britain). Below this, though, the distributional pattern for income and spending changes are very different. The next highest growth in incomes occurs around the 25th percentile, and income growth falls as we move from the 25th to the 80th percentile, implying an equalising of incomes in this part of the income distribution. For spending, the fastest growth has again been near the top of

the overall distribution, but there is no obvious equalisation in the middle of the spending distribution.

We will examine trends in relative poverty measured with both income and expenditure in the next section, but it is important to realise that such poverty rates are merely another way of showing how relative incomes and spending in the bottom half of the distribution have changed. Having seen Figure 2.2(b), we should not be surprised if the recent trends in income and spending poverty were quite different.

Comparing relative poverty measures based on income and expenditure

One very common way to measure poverty is to count the number of individuals whose household income falls below some poverty line: this is the method preferred by the current government for the majority of its child poverty targets[2], and is also used to define a number of

---

[2] The child poverty target for 2004/05 was solely based this way. The target for 2010/11 contains two income-based targets, based on the 60% median income poverty line, and an as yet unspecified target for material deprivation. The authors have previously argued that of these three components of the 2010/11 target, the measure defined in terms of relative income will be the hardest to reduce (see Brewer et al, 2004).

Figure 2.2: Income and expenditure growth across the distribution

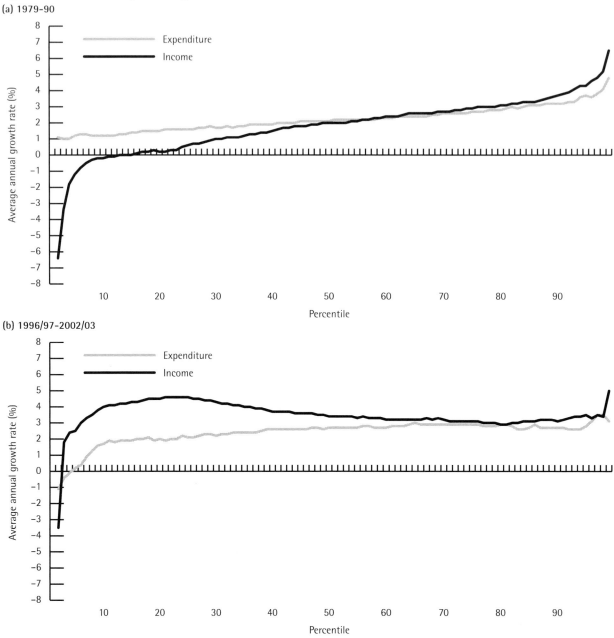

(a) 1979-90

(b) 1996/97-2002/03

Notes: Figures show average annual growth rates *at* each percentile point of the income or spending distribution, not the average *within* each point.

Source: Authors' calculations based on FRS and FES/EFS

indicators in their annual poverty audit. Such measures have been criticised because the poverty line is arbitrary, and need not correspond to what society nor experts think should be the poverty line[3]. However, given this arbitrariness, it is no more arbitrary to construct a similar measure of poverty that uses expenditure, rather than income: under such a measure, individuals are classified as poor if they live in households that spend less

than some expenditure-based poverty line. As is common in the UK (and indeed the European Union) when measuring income poverty, we can define a relative measure of spending poverty by setting the poverty line as defined as 60% of the median individual's expenditure[4]. An individual is counted as poor if the expenditure of their household is below this 60% median spending threshold.

---

[3] See, for instance, Parker (1998, 2000, 2002) for examples of poverty lines based on the budget standards methodology, and Deeming (2005) for a review.

[4] In both income and spending poverty measures, household income and spending is adjusted for household size and composition: we use the McClements scale throughout (see Chapter 1 and Appendix 6 of DWP, 2005).

Figure 2.3: Income and expenditure poverty rates (1961–2002/03)

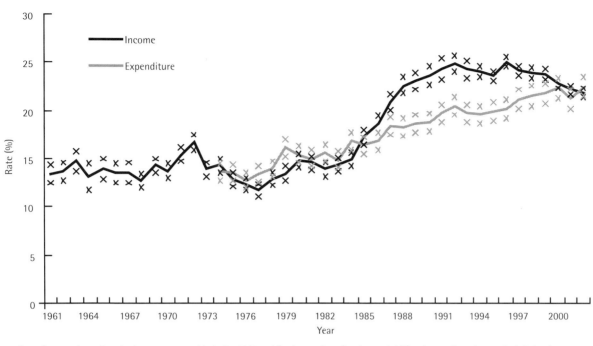

Notes: Data are drawn for calendar years up to and including 1992, and fiscal years thereafter. Income is AHC and expenditure does not include housing.

Source: Authors' calculations from FES and FRS (various years)

Figure 2.3 shows relative income and expenditure poverty rates since 1961, where poverty is defined as living in a household with less than 60% of the contemporaneous median income or expenditure (95% confidence intervals around the rate are also drawn, reflecting uncertainties due to sampling error). Table 2.1 shows some examples of how this way of defining poverty translates into poverty lines (in £/week) for various families, and Table 2.2 gives more detail for the trends since 1996/97.

We turn first to income poverty, where the trends have also been widely documented elsewhere: in the 1960s and 1970s, income poverty rates were virtually flat at around 12 to 15%. In the early 1980s, there was a sustained and dramatic rise in the poverty rate, to a new peak of 25% in 1992. Since then, rates have been declining steadily but gently: by 2002/03, the poverty rate had fallen to 22%, its lowest value since 1987. Statistical tests of whether changes in poverty rates over time are significantly different suggest that the 2002/03 value was significantly less than that recorded in 1989 and in 1996/97. Although the recent fall in poverty is biggest when focusing on the 60% of median poverty line, it is also apparent for the other income poverty lines shown in Table 2.2.

For expenditure, the story is very different. Since our measure begins, in 1974, the poverty rate based on spending has been rising continually, although its rate of growth was not as fast over the 1980s as the growth in income poverty. From a low point of 13% in 1976, the rate rose to 18% by the end of the 1980s and further to 22% by the end of the 1990s. A decline in 2001/02 was reversed in 2002/03 such that at the end of our period, expenditure poverty reached a new record peak of just over 22%, and the rate was higher than the income poverty rate for the first time since 1984. A standard statistical test reveals that the fact that the expenditure poverty rate in 2002/03 exceeded the 1996/97 rate that Labour inherited is very unlikely to be due to sampling error[5]. Again, although the rise is biggest on the 60% of median measure, a rise is also apparent for the other expenditure poverty lines shown in Table 2.2.

The recent story on poverty is therefore very different depending on whether one looks at household income or expenditure. With an income measure of poverty, the current government can claim considerable success in

---

[5] A full breakdown of the statistical significance of changes in income and poverty rates across time is available from the authors.

Table 2.1: Example poverty lines in 2002/03

Family type	Weekly income (AHC) (£)			Weekly expenditure (not including housing) (£)		
	50% median	60% median	70% median	50% median	60% median	70% median
Couple with no children	144	173	202	132	158	184
Single individual	79	95	111	72	87	101
Couple with one child aged 8	177	213	248	162	194	226
Couple with two children aged 1 and 3	180	216	252	164	197	230
Lone parent with one child aged 8	112	135	157	103	123	144
Lone parent with two children aged 1 and 3	115	138	162	105	126	147

Source: Authors' calculations based on FRS, 2002/03, and EFS, 2002/03

Table 2.2: Relative poverty rates using income and expenditure (1996/97–2002/03)

	% of the population						
	Income (AHC)			Expenditure (not including housing costs)			
	50% median	60% median	70% median	50% median	60% median	70% median	Population (million)
1996/97	16.1	24.8	31.6	12.9	19.9	27.8	55.6
1997/98	15.8	23.8	30.5	14.1	20.9	28.2	55.7
1998/99	15.6	23.7	30.4	14.3	21.3	29.2	55.9
1999/2000	15.4	23.5	30.5	14.8	21.5	28.6	56.1
2000/01	14.7	22.6	29.6	14.3	22.0	29.3	56.2
2001/02	14.3	21.9	29.3	13.6	21.0	28.6	56.4
2002/03	14.2	21.6	29.5	14.9	22.2	29.3	56.6
Change:							
Since 1996/97	−1.9	−3.2	−2.1	+2.0	+2.3	+1.5	
Since 1998/99	−1.4	−2.1	−0.9	+0.6	+0.9	+0.1	

Note: Reported changes may not equal the differences between the corresponding percentages due to rounding.
Source: Authors' calculations based on FRS and FES, various years. Population totals are from the HBAI dataset

reducing poverty from 25% in 1996/97 to 22% in 2002/03, a fall of 12% or 3 percentage points. But if we switch attention to expenditure, poverty over the same period rose from 20% to 22%, a rise of 12% or 2.3 percentage points. In other words, there has been an equivalent *rise* in expenditure poverty to match the fall in income poverty since the current Labour government came to power.

As well as the overall poverty rate, it is important to look at rates of child poverty, particularly given the prominence attached to it by the Labour government[6]. The trends are shown in Figure 2.4 and in Table 2.3.

As with poverty in the whole population, the trends in child poverty are markedly different when one considers expenditure rather than income. As with poverty overall, the income poverty rate for children was broadly stable through the 1960s and 1970s and rose rapidly in the 1980s to a high point of 33% in 1993/94.

---

[6] The government has an explicit target for child poverty in 2010/11, and aims to eradicate child poverty by 2020 (or at least to reduce the British rate to levels comparable with those in Scandinavian countries: see DWP, 2003, para 70).

Figure 2.4: Trends in child poverty (1961–2002/03)

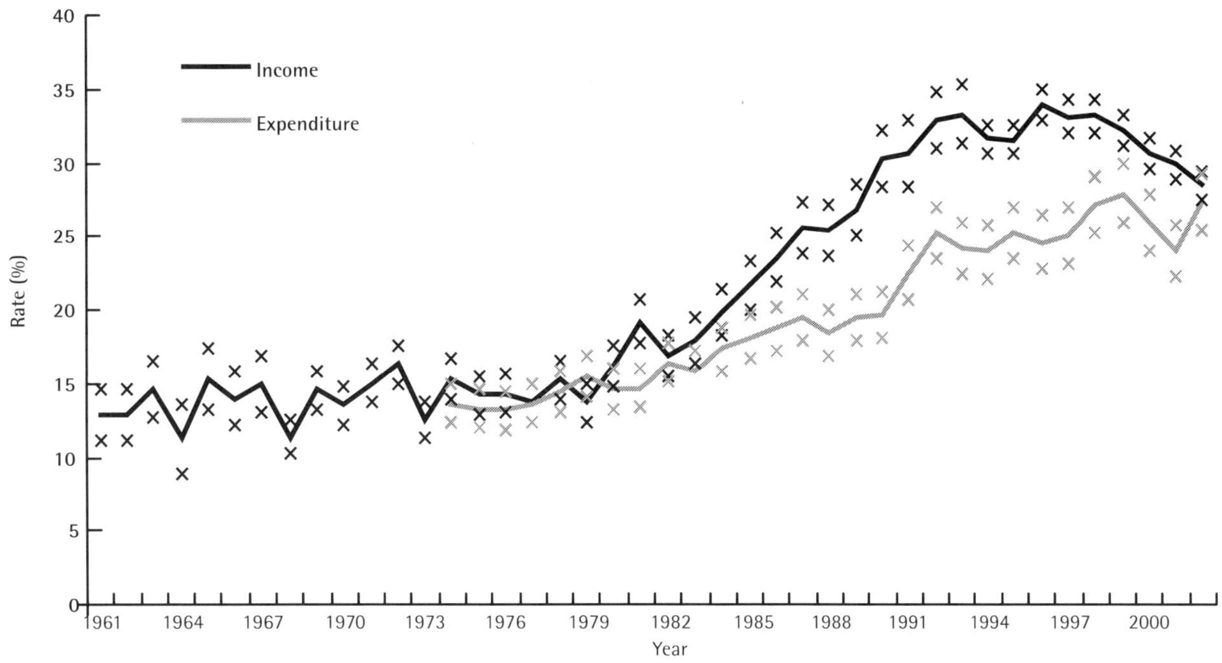

Notes: Data are drawn for calendar years up to and including 1992, and fiscal years thereafter. Income is AHC and expenditure does not include housing.

Source: Author's calculations from FES and FRS (various years)

Table 2.3: Relative child poverty: percentage of children living in households with incomes below various fractions of median income

| | % of children | | | | | | |
| | Income (AHC) | | | Expenditure (not including housing costs) | | | |
	50% median	60% median	70% median	50% median	60% median	70% median	Population (million)
1996/97	22.9	33.3	41.2	16.1	24.6	34.3	12.7
1997/98	22.9	32.4	40.1	17.7	25.1	33.3	12.7
1998/99	22.7	32.5	40.4	18.7	27.1	37.0	12.7
1999/2000	21.8	31.9	40.2	19.7	27.9	35.9	12.7
2000/01	19.7	30.3	38.6	17.2	26.0	33.9	12.7
2001/02	19.3	29.6	38.3	15.8	24.1	32.9	12.6
2002/03	19.0	28.3	37.6	18.9	27.3	35.5	12.6
Change:							
Since 1996/97	*–3.9*	*–5.0*	*–3.6*	*+2.8*	*+2.7*	*+1.2*	
Since 1998/99	*–3.7*	*–4.2*	*–2.8*	*+0.2*	*+0.2*	*–1.5*	

Note: Reported changes may not equal the differences between the corresponding percentages due to rounding.

Source: Authors' calculations based on FRS and FES, various years. Population totals are from the HBAI dataset

Since then, the trend has been downwards, and the decline has been more pronounced among children than the population as a whole: since 1996/97, the child poverty rate based on incomes has fallen from 34% to 29%, a fall of 16% or 5 percentage points.

Yet again, the picture is different if we switch focus to expenditure. There has been an almost continuous rise in the expenditure poverty rate for children, and although child poverty on this measure did not grow as fast over the 1980s as the income poverty rate, there were particularly sharp increases in the late 1980s and early 1990s. The expenditure poverty rate peaked at 28% in 1999/2000, after which there were two years of sharp declines, taking the rate back down to 24%. Most of this appears to have been undone in the 2002/03 data, with the rate rising again to 27%, close to its old peak. Between 1996/97 and 2002/03, expenditure poverty for children rose by 11%, or 3 percentage points, an amount which is

statistically greater than 0 (however, the rate in 2001/02 was *not* statistically significantly different from that in 1996/97). Unless the rise in 2002/03 proves to be a one-off, it seems that child poverty based on household expenditure has not been reduced.

Figure 2.5 and Table 2.4 show what has happened to poverty rates among pensioners.

Figure 2.5: Trends in pensioner poverty (1961-2002/03)

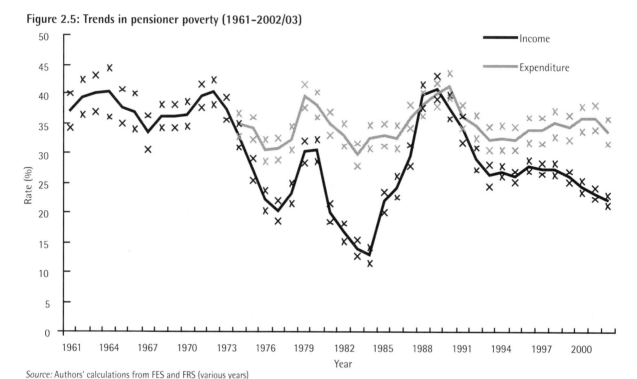

Source: Authors' calculations from FES and FRS (various years)

Table 2.4: Relative pensioner poverty: percentage of pensioners in households with incomes below various fractions of median income

	% of the pensioner population						
	Income (AHC)			Expenditure (not including housing costs)			
	50% median	60% median	70% median	50% median	60% median	70% median	Population (million)
1996/97	12.1	27.9	39.2	23.5	34.0	44.3	9.9
1997/98	12.5	27.4	38.4	22.9	33.8	44.2	10.0
1998/99	12.6	27.3	38.1	24.3	35.0	45.4	10.0
1999/2000	12.1	26.1	37.2	23.9	34.4	43.2	10.0
2000/01	11.3	24.4	35.8	23.9	35.8	45.9	10.1
2001/02	11.1	23.2	36.6	23.9	36.1	45.6	10.1
2002/03	10.5	22.1	36.7	23.0	33.7	43.9	10.2
Change:							
Since 1996/97	*−1.6*	*−5.8*	*−2.5*	*−0.5*	*−0.3*	*−0.4*	
Since 1998/99	*−2.1*	*−5.2*	*−1.4*	*−1.3*	*−1.3*	*−1.5*	

Note: Reported changes may not equal the differences between the corresponding percentages due to rounding.

Source: Authors' calculations based on FRS, various years. Population totals are from the HBAI dataset

Three striking features are evident from Figure 2.5:

- Pensioner poverty rates are considerably higher when measured using expenditure than when using income; for other groups, the two rates are much closer, and slightly higher, for income.
- There is a remarkable degree of volatility in the pensioner income poverty rate that is not reflected to the same degree in spending poverty rates[7]. The volatility of income poverty among pensioners seems to be related to the economic cycle: because pensioner incomes are largely fixed (in either nominal or real terms) through state benefits or occupational pensions, pensioner poverty tends to fall in times of recession, because pensioners get better off relative to the working-age population, and it tends to rise when the economy is growing strongly[8].
- Poverty rates measured by spending have not fallen much in recent years – indeed, until the latest data in 2002/03, they had not fallen at all – in a period when there has been a large and unprecedented (given the position in the economic cycle) decline in pensioner income poverty. In Chapter 4 we attempt to assess some of the factors behind the recent diverging trends for pensioners, by examining the extent to which pensioners have altered their spending levels and patterns as a result of the large increases to their means-tested benefits entitlements in recent years.

Box 2.1 assesses how sensitive our findings are to measurement choices related to housing expenditure. Since many pensioners are owner-occupiers, with relatively low housing costs, this issue is particularly important for considering poverty among this group.

Our focus on child and pensioner poverty follows the government's own stated priorities, but it is important to look at poverty rates among working-age adults without children as well: Figure 2.6 overleaf shows income and expenditure poverty rates for working-age adults without children[9].

Trends in income poverty for working-age adults without children are different from those for pensioners and children: income poverty rates rose rapidly in the 1980s (from a low starting point), but then continued to rise in the first half of the 1990s even as child poverty rates were stabilising and pensioner poverty rates falling. In the late 1990s, income poverty among working-age adults without children was broadly unchanged. Expenditure poverty rates for this group have risen almost continuously since our data begins (1974). In statistical terms, there has been no significant change in income poverty among working-age adults with no children since the early 1990s, but the 2002/03 spending poverty rate is the highest ever recorded, and significantly above that recorded in any year other than 1997/98 and 2000/01.

Understanding the differences in poverty trends between income and spending measures

Essentially, this analysis shows us that the changes in the distribution of income that led to the rapidly rising income poverty rates in the 1980s and falling income poverty rates over the late 1990s and early 2000s were not

---

[7] We might wonder if this is an artefact of the choice of the poverty line at 60% of median income or spending in a given year. For example, pensioners might be clustered around the 60% median income line such that relatively small changes can produce large swings in poverty rates, but may not be clustered around the 60% spending line. Repeating the analysis with poverty lines at 50% and 70% of income and spending does not change the result that income poverty (with a general downward trend) is more volatile than spending poverty (with 0 trend), however.

[8] The strong economic growth from the mid-to-late 1990s did not result in a large upturn in pensioner income poverty, perhaps as a result of deliberate benefit reforms aimed at the poorest pensioners by the current government. Indeed, pensioner income poverty rates in 2002/03 were significantly lower than even those just two years earlier in 2000/01 (see Brewer et al, 2005 and Goodman et al, 2003).

[9] Official publications on poverty split the population into three groups: children, pensioners, and working-age adults. However, because the poverty rate of working-age adults with children follows a very similar trend to that of children (by construction, because the HBAI methodology places each individual in a given household at the same point in the income distribution), it is more interesting to look at the poverty rate of working-age adults who are not living with dependent children.

Box 2.1: Does the inclusion of housing change our findings?

Our main analysis focuses on trends in expenditure excluding housing. We have chosen to use this measure of partial rather than total spending because standard measures of housing expenditure do not adequately reflect housing consumption. In particular, housing expenditure provides a very poor measure of consumption for homeowners who own their properties outright, many of whom are pensioners. These households typically have very low housing spending but potentially much higher housing consumption.

We have assessed the sensitivity of our findings about living standards and poverty by also using an alternative approach to measuring housing spending. Rather than simply excluding housing from our expenditure measure, we have also derived a measure of total expenditure including housing consumption, using an imputed measure of housing consumption for all households, including owner-occupiers. This imputed measure is based on our best estimate of the rent that would be charged for an equivalent property in the private rented sector.

We find that including imputed housing consumption in total expenditure means that:

- spending poverty rates are somewhat lower compared to when housing is excluded; but
- this does not affect our main conclusions about the trends in spending poverty over time.

Our sensitivity analysis also shows that imputing housing consumption rather than just including housing expenditures in total spending is very important. If we include housing expenditures rather than imputed housing consumption, it appears that there have been bigger rises in spending poverty over recent years, particularly among pensioners. However, this apparent upward trend in poverty among pensioners seems to be driven by an increase in the number of pensioners with very low housing expenditure due to owner-occupation.

Housing is, of course, not the only good for which the consumption and expenditure elements are not the same. All durable goods exhibit the same property – providing a stream of consumption benefits after an initial expenditure outlay. Unfortunately, there is no easy way to repeat the above analysis for durables since there is rarely information on a rental market for durables from which we could impute a rental equivalent value. For more details on our methods and findings please contact the authors.

Figure 2.6: Trends in poverty among working-age adults without children (1961-2002/03)

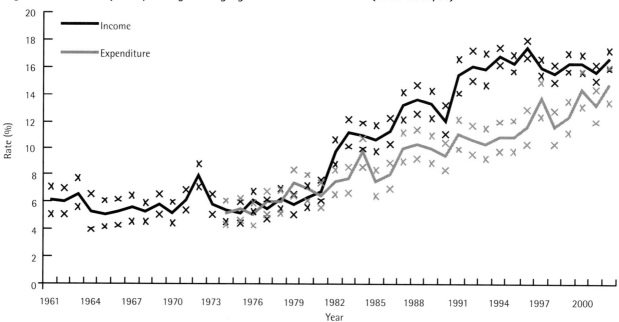

Source: Authors' calculations from FES and FRS (various years)

replicated in the distribution of spending. In particular, in recent years the lowest spenders have not been catching up with the median spender, even though some of the lowest incomes have been catching up with the median income.

It is important to try to understand what explains these differences in the trends for income poverty and spending poverty. Below we discuss three potential explanations:

- One concern would be if these differences in trends were just due to changes in the way that spending is measured, perhaps due to changes in the way that people spend their money, or how it is recorded in household surveys. For example, a growing 'lumpiness' of expenditure – with more being spent on durables and less on non-durables, for example – would lead to an apparent, but artificial, rise in spending poverty. This is because we would tend to see growing numbers of people recording low spending in any given period, even though living standards had not changed. However, we are confident that this is not an important phenomenon. First, spending on 'lumpy' items (like furniture) is recorded over a three-month time horizon, from which a two-week equivalent spending amount is derived (it has been collected this way since the late 1980s). There is no apparent difference in trends in inequality of expenditure when retrospective recall items are used to count spending on these items or when only purchases within the two-week diary window are included. Second, evidence on spending trends suggests that the shift in spending patterns has been away from non-durable goods towards services, and that the share of spending devoted to durables has remained relatively stable over time (see Blow et al, 2004).

- One explanation that has often been suggested for different trends in the distribution of income and spending relates to the degree of transitory variation in incomes: as we have shown, spending poverty rose over the 1980s, but income poverty grew faster. A number of commentators have suggested that this is because there was both an increase in permanent, long-term income differences, and also a growth in transitory, short-term income differences through a rise in temporary unemployment, fluctuations in hours worked and more reliability on uncertain income sources, such as self-employment[10]. According to this line of thinking, the growth in spending poverty over this time reflects the increase in inequality only in permanent incomes, while the greater growth in income poverty over the same time reflects the changes to both permanent and transitory incomes. Extending this logic to the experience of the late 1990s would suggest that even though short-run, transitory income differences have been reduced (for example, through increases to means-tested benefits and tax credits for some groups of the population, leading to falls in income poverty), there has been no similar reduction in long-run permanent differences, which are reflected in the still-rising rates of spending poverty. Such logic also suggests that policy measures to improve individuals' long-run earnings potential (for example, through education interventions early in life) are more likely to be effective in reducing spending poverty than simply increasing financial transfers to households through the tax and benefit system.

- An alternative explanation to this would be if there had been systematic changes in saving and borrowing behaviour, unrelated to any change in the balance between permanent and transitory incomes discussed above. For example, our findings would be consistent with a growth in the long-run savings rate of low-income families in recent years; however, assessing this lies outside the scope of this report.

Of course, all of these could be partially responsible for the changes we observe; more research is required beyond the descriptive analysis provided here to understand the true causation.

---

[10] For example, see Blundell and Preston (1998).

Who is considered poor when using expenditure to measure poverty?

As well as differences in trends in poverty over time, Table 2.5 shows that who we think of as poor differs depending on whether income or spending is used as the preferred measure of living standards. Table 2.5 shows poverty rates and 'poverty ratios' for various demographic groups[11].

Some groups are much more likely to be in poverty than others: lone parents and workless households (whether sick, unoccupied or unemployed) all have poverty ratios in excess

of 2, and poverty rates approaching or above 50% whether one looks at income or spending poverty. By contrast, some groups tend to have very low incidences of poverty irrespective of our measure: couples without children and employees, for example.

Of particular interest, however, are those groups where income poverty rates and ratios differ from spending poverty. For example, in households where the head is self-employed, income poverty rates are well above spending poverty rates (23% compared to 13%), and those who are seeking work are more likely to be poor when looking at their income than at their spending. It is highly likely that the discrepancy between the poverty rates for these two groups arises because these groups are relatively likely to be experiencing temporarily low income, but are able to access savings or can borrow and so can smooth out the short-run drop in income. In other words, because a temporary decline in incomes has little impact on the household's average or

[11] The poverty ratio is defined as the ratio of the proportion of each group in the poverty population to their proportion in the whole population. A group which made up 20% of those in poverty but just 10% of everyone would have a poverty ratio of 2.0: a ratio above 1 suggests the group is over-represented among those in poverty; a ratio below 1 suggests it is under-represented.

Table 2.5: Poverty breakdown by demographic group (2002-03)

	Poverty rates (%)		Poverty ratios	
	Income	Spending	Income	Spending
Type of family:				
Single with children	51.4	48.1	2.36	2.16
Couple with children	19.1	18.0	0.88	0.81
Pensioner couples	23.1	29.3	1.06	1.32
Pensioner singles	19.7	42.1	0.90	1.89
Single no children	24.0	20.4	1.10	0.92
Couple no children	11.9	10.8	0.54	0.49
Number of children:				
None	18.8	20.9	0.86	0.94
One	22.4	17.2	1.03	0.77
Two	22.3	20.8	1.02	0.94
Three or more	35.7	39.5	1.64	1.78
Working status:				
No worker	58.9	50.4	2.70	2.27
At least one worker	11.3	13.8	0.52	0.62
All retired	21.9	34.8	1.01	1.57
Employment status:				
Employee	9.6	13.6	0.44	0.61
Self-employed	22.6	12.6	1.04	0.57
Seeking work	70.1	50.4	3.22	2.26
Sick or injured	53.8	46.8	2.47	2.10
Retired	21.9	32.6	1.01	1.46
Unoccupied/other	57.1	49.4	2.62	2.22

Note: Poverty ratios defined as proportion of group in poverty ÷ proportion of group in the population.

permanent income, their spending hardly changes even though their short-run income is very low. This does not mean we should not be concerned about income poverty among self-employed people or those seeking work; while for some of these people low income will be a brief state, for others it will be a long-term problem for which the policy implications will be very different.

There is another group where income poverty rates differ from spending poverty, but in the opposite direction to self-employed and unemployed people: the income poverty rate among single pensioners is 20%, but the spending poverty rate is more than double that, at 42% (among households where all adults are retired, the income poverty rate is 22% and the expenditure poverty rate is 35%). The difference between the income and spending poverty rates for pensioners, which is not a new phenomenon, is usually put down to the fact that many low-income pensioners are not spending all of their income, even though they have little income relative to society[12]. Our contribution to this discussion is given in Chapter 4, where we examine the extent to which some low-income pensioners have altered their spending patterns as a result of the large increases to their means-tested benefits entitlements in recent years.

Looking at changes in the composition of the poor over time, Figures 2.7 and 2.8 show the composition of the population defined as being in relative income poverty and spending poverty respectively, where we have classified people into four broad demographic groups: people without children (whether singles or couples) below pension age, lone parents, families with children, and pensioners, and where we measure relative poverty using income and expenditure, as in the first section to this chapter.

Two strong trends emerge from Figures 2.7 and 2.8[13]:

- *Pensioners:* while the share of pensioners among the income-poor is much lower now than it was, there has been a much smaller decline in the share of pensioners among the spending-poor. So, while pensioners made up about 40% of the income-poor in the early 1960s (around 5 percentage points out of 13), this has dropped to less than 20% (around 4 percentage points out of 22) in recent years, despite the fact that the share of pensioners in the total population has risen considerably. On the other hand, pensioners still make up nearly 30% of the spending-poor. There are just as many poor pensioners now as there were in 1974.

- *Lone parents:* as with income poverty, the proportion of the spending-poor who are lone parents has risen over time. This is partly because of the rise in the number of lone parents in the population over this time, but is also due to the change in the composition of the lone-parent population (to on average younger, less well-educated, adults).

---

[12] See, for example, Goodman et al (1997).

[13] It should be noted that changes over time are driven both by changes in the relative size of the demographic groups in the population, as well as by changes in the relative levels of income or spending within the groups.

Figure 2.7: Demographic breakdown of income poverty (1961–2002/03)

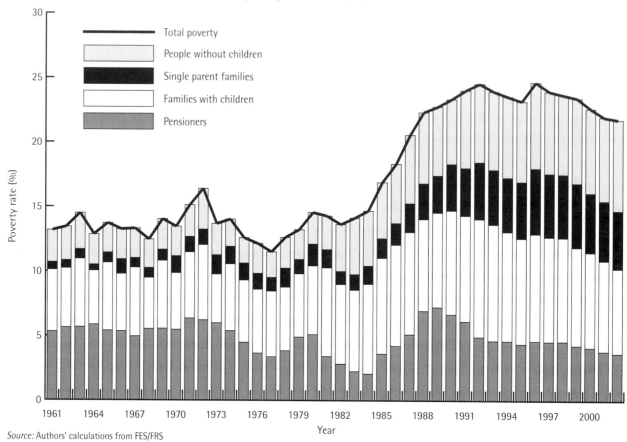

Source: Authors' calculations from FES/FRS

Figure 2.8: Demographic breakdown of spending poverty (1974–2002/03)

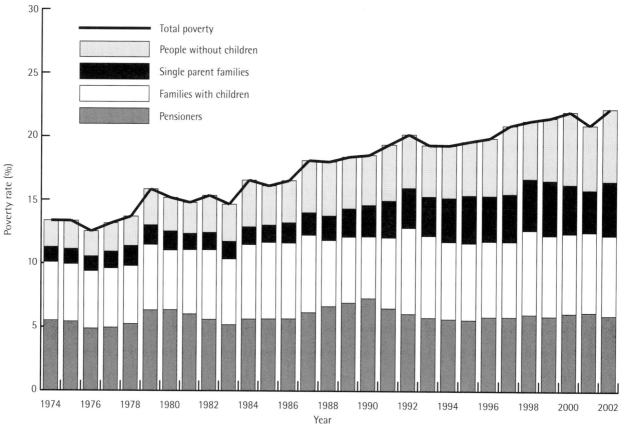

Source: Authors' calculations from FES/FRS

Conclusions

This chapter has shown that some stylised facts about living standards are true whether we consider income or spending: real living standards have, in general, risen over time and across generations, and this is reflected in increases in both the average income and average spending of British households.

Similarly, relative poverty rates rose over much of the 1980s, whether we consider income or spending, as inequality widened across both the income and spending distributions. However, the rise in income poverty was much bigger than the rise in spending poverty. In more recent years, families on the lowest incomes have, in general, seen their incomes rise faster than middle-income households, thereby reducing income poverty rates. This has not been the case for the lowest spenders, and spending poverty rates have continued to rise: across the whole population, the proportion of individuals living in households who spend less than 60% of the median has risen from 20% to 22%, a rise of 12% (or 2.3 percentage points), or a rise of exactly the same magnitude as the proportional fall in the income poverty rate, which dropped by 12% over this time.

Between Labour coming to power in 1997 and 2002/03, the child poverty rate has risen from 25% to around 27% (a rise of 11%) using expenditure, while it fell from around 33% to 28% (a fall of around 15%) using income over the same period. Pensioner poverty has remained roughly unchanged on spending, but income poverty has fallen rapidly.

We have made some tentative conclusions about what might cause these differences in income and spending poverty trends. Although not conclusive, our findings suggest that recent income improvements among poorer households perhaps reflect temporary rather than permanent income changes, and are therefore not reflected in the distribution of expenditure. In Chapter 4 we consider this hypothesis more directly, by considering whether pensioners have increased their spending as a result of recent benefit reforms.

Income and expenditure behaviour of the same households

As well as assessing trends in poverty using household spending as a measure of well-being, it is also useful to use household expenditure to help us understand more about the living standards of households with the very lowest incomes. We do this first by considering the overlap between income and spending poverty, and second by considering how the expenditure of the lowest-income households compares to households higher up the income scale. For this, we need to examine the income and spending of the same households (see Chapter 1 for more detail on the measures of income and spending used).

The overlap between income and spending poverty

In this section we consider what proportion of those who are deemed to be poor according to their income are also poor on the spending measure.

Figure 3.1 below shows the extent of overlap (using Venn diagrams) in three years: 2002/03 (the latest year of data), 1996/97 (the figures inherited by Labour) and, for historical comparison, 1974 (the first year of data). In each figure, the total number in income poverty is given by adding the figure in the left-hand circle to that in the section where the circles overlap; total spending poverty is given by adding the figure in the right-hand circle with that in the overlap.

In the latest year of data (2002/03), of the approximately 13 million people deemed poor according to their income, only 56% are also deemed to be poor on account of their expenditure. Similarly, of the approximately 12.5 million people in expenditure poverty, only 58% are also in income poverty. These two states are clearly distinct from one another, although this has typically been the case since 1974, when around 52% of the income-poor were also spending-poor, and 57% of the spending-poor were also income-poor.

Figure 3.1: The overlap between spending and income poverty (2002/03, 1996/97 and 1974)

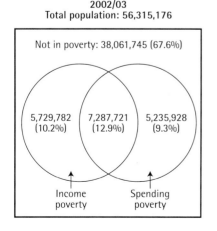

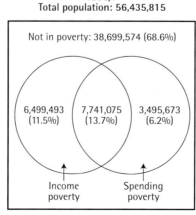

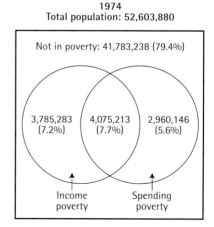

Figure 3.2: Expenditure among the lowest income half of households (2001/02–2002/03)

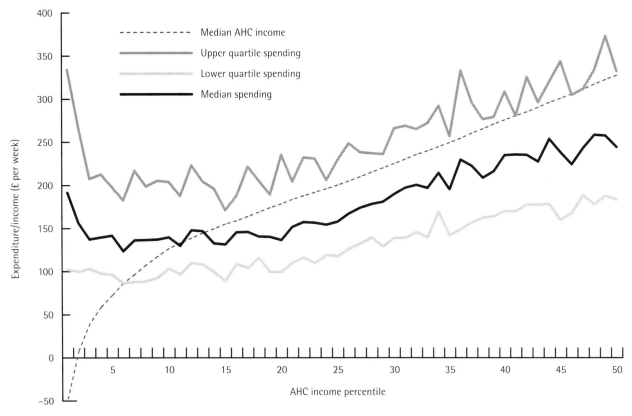

Notes: The median and quartiles of spending are drawn from the within-income-percentile distributions; that is, of the households in the bottom income percentile, median expenditure per week was £192, and the upper and lower quartiles were £334 and £102. Among those households, median income was –£47/week.

Source: Authors' calculations from FES/EFS

Spending across the income distribution

In order to understand the reason for this lack of overlap better, Figure 3.2 shows spending levels among individuals in the bottom half of the income distribution[1]. The graph has divided the population into 100 equally sized groups (percentile groups) according to their real income, and plotted the median, upper and lower quartile of expenditure for the bottom 50 percentiles (that is, the lowest-income half of the population). The dotted line shows the median income for each percentile: by construction, this rises as we move up the percentiles.

It is clear that most households at the very bottom of the income distribution – among the poorest 2% – spend more than those further up the income distribution (having adjusted for

household size and composition). The poorest 1% of households spend, on average, more than any percentile up to the 31st. We call this phenomenon the expenditure 'tick' (referring to the shape of the line showing median expenditure against income percentile, that is, a ✓).

The presence of the tick suggests that, for some of those at the very bottom of the income distribution, a recorded very low income should not be taken as a sign of more general lack of resources. There are several explanations that could account for the presence of the expenditure tick:

• It might reflect the fact that some individuals experience very low income for a relatively short period of time, but that they maintain their spending at some sort of long-run level: for example, someone between jobs (who could have a 0 or very low income if measured over a sufficiently short period), or someone making a loss in their self-employment business (which would count as a negative income), may well be able to maintain their expenditure so that their

---

[1] This combines households from the last two years of data, 2001/02 and 2002/03, in order to obtain a relatively large sample size.

Table 3.1: Expenditure 'tick' summary data

	1st income percentile			1st income percentile median expenditure as % of ...		
Years	Median expenditure	Median income	Next equivalent percentile[a]	10th percentile spending	50th percentile spending	90th percentile spending
1974-75	114.59	47.52	15th	105.1	59.5	40.4
1981-82	143.65	39.71	38th	138.2	89.0	51.7
1991-92	192.87	−43.55	42nd	158.8	84.2	54.7
2001-02	191.6	−47.10	31st	137.1	78.4	39.5

Note: [a]The next income percentile with the same or a higher median expenditure value as the bottom income percentile.

living standard is fairly constant. The fact that some people within the bottom percentile have a *negative* AHC income (reflecting the fact that their housing costs exceed their BHC [before housing costs] incomes) is suggestive of this – in the long run, a negative income is not sustainable.

- It may reflect that income is being measured with error among some people in the FES/EFS, so that those with apparently very low income actually have much higher short-run income than it appears[2].

It is difficult, with the data available, to infer the relative importance of each: it is likely that a combination of both issues is at work. For example, around one quarter of the bottom 2% of the income distribution consists of individuals who are seeking work or are self-employed, suggesting that their incomes may be transitorily low. However, nearly 60% are reported as unoccupied, long-term sick, or retired, while 10% are employed. Whatever the cause, our analysis suggests that among those with the very lowest reported incomes, living standards are not in general as low as their incomes suggest.

The expenditure 'ticks' have not remained constant over time. Table 3.1 reports median

expenditure and income for the lowest income 1%, the next income percentile with a higher median expenditure than the poorest 1%, and the median expenditure for the poorest 1% as a percentage of the median expenditure at various points in the income distribution.

The height of the tick grew between 1974-75 and 1991-92, but is now smaller. For example, in 1974-75, households in the bottom income percentile spent 60% as much as those at the middle of the income distribution; by 1991-92, they spent 84% as much. In 1974-75, median expenditure in the 2nd to 14th income percentiles was lower than that in the 1st; by 1991-92, one had to go up to the 42nd income percentile to find households who spent as much as those in the 1st percentile.

It is also uncertain what has caused the variation over time in the size of the tick, although there is an academic literature suggesting that the transitory components of household incomes in the UK and US have become more important over time, and this could increase the size of the expenditure tick.

Interestingly, there is no visible tick if we plot the relationship the other way round: people at the very bottom of the spending distribution tend to have lower incomes than households who spend more (see Figure 3.3; the relationship looks very similar in other years and is not shown here). Although this is not a definitive test, this does suggest that one would get a more reliable picture of who those are with the lowest standards of living by examining those recorded at the bottom of the spending distribution than one would if one looked among those recorded at the bottom of the income distribution.

---

[2] Although most people would be happy to accept that household surveys measure income with error, it is worth noting that if this were simply random noise (otherwise known as 'classical measurement error') then a plot of expenditure against mis-measured income would still slope upwards. For measurement error to change the slope of a plot, it needs to have a non-classical form. This suggests that particular sorts of people or income levels are more likely to be measured with error than others, rather than it being random across the population.

Figure 3.3: Income among the half of households that spent the least (2001/02–2002/03)

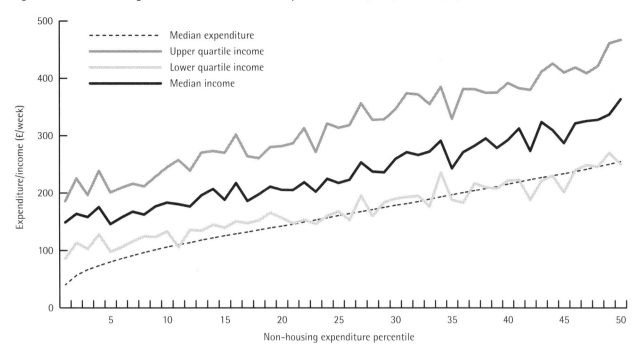

Note: The median and quartiles of income are drawn from the within-spending-percentile distributions.

Source: Authors' calculations from FES/EFS

Conclusions

The analysis of this chapter suggests that among those with the very lowest living standards in our society, spending rather than income may be a better measure of these living standards: in particular, the lowest 2% of the income distribution have higher expenditure than we would expect from their incomes alone. Thus a more reliable picture of who is genuinely very poor may be obtained from an examination of the bottom of the spending distribution rather than the income distribution.

This is relevant for the government's aspiration for child poverty to be abolished by 2020, now understood to mean to be among the best in Europe, with a rate between 5% and 10%. Our evidence reinforces the government's view that it would be impossible for child poverty recorded using the current methodology ever to fall to 0. Our evidence also suggests that the target probably escapes the territory in which incomes are particularly poorly measured, although it does mean that future successful anti-poverty policies may not be reflected at the very bottom of the income distribution.

4

The effect of increased benefit entitlements on pensioner spending

In this chapter we assess whether the recent increases in means-tested benefits directed towards pensioners have affected pensioner spending levels, and patterns of spending among pensioners. Our focus on pensioners is motivated by the finding that expenditure poverty rates have not fallen among pensioners in recent years (see Figure 2.5), despite the fact that pensioners are one of the main groups to have benefited from increases in benefits and tax credits since 1997, and that income poverty rates have fallen substantially. Pensioners are also an interesting group because pensioners on low incomes tend to be even lower spenders (again, see Chapter 2).

One explanation for the divergence in income and spending poverty trends would be if low-income pensioners had not increased their spending in response to their increased benefit entitlements. Addressing this question is particularly important, since it allows us to test the effectiveness of income supplementation as a policy for improving the well-being of this group.

The chapter first describes the recent changes to policy and shows how they have affected pensioners in different ways depending on their age and their income. We then compare trends in income and spending for these groups, before presenting a more formal statistical analysis of the changes. Other research has examined how the spending

habits of low-income families with children in the UK have changed in response to the recent benefit increases directed at them, so we do not consider families with children, or indeed any other population groups, here (Gregg et al, 2005).

Recent tax and benefit changes affecting pensioners

The increases in benefit entitlements for pensioners during Labour's period in office, but particularly since 1999, have been one of the important contributors to falling pensioner income poverty in recent years. The series of significant increases to benefits for those aged 60 or over have led to an estimated real terms increase in public expenditure on benefits targeted on pensioners of 33%[1]. The main reforms since 1997 have been:

- occasional real terms increases in the Basic State Pension (such as the £5/week increase in 2001);
- introduction of (1999) and increases in (various years) Winter Fuel Payments;

---

[1]   Nominal spending on benefits targeted on pensioners rose from around £40.0 billion in 1996/97 to an estimated £64.6 billion in 2004/05. See Tables 1 and 2 at www.dwp.gov.uk/asd/asd4/medium_term.asp.

- introduction of the Minimum Income Guarantee (MIG) (April 2001) and Pension Credit (October 2003), with increases in value/generosity over time;
- the equalisation of three tiers of pensioner premia in Income Support (IS), Housing Benefit (HB) and Council Tax Benefit (CTB) at the highest rate for pensioners (April 2001);
- a series of ad hoc help to older pensioners, supposedly justified by the growth in Council Tax bills (winter 2004 and 2005).

All of these reforms have meant additional income entitlements for pensioners. However, despite these increases in entitlements, Chapter 2 showed that spending poverty among pensioners has not fallen. A natural question to ask is, therefore, whether the increases to pensioner incomes from higher benefit entitlement have led to higher spending by pensioners?

Such questions can be difficult to answer, since it is impossible to observe what would have happened to pensioners' spending in the absence of the policy reforms. However, not all pensioners have benefited equally from the policy changes outlined above, and this allows us some insight into how the policy changes might be related to changes in spending. For example:

- Many of the increases in benefits have been to means-tested benefits, meaning that they have raised the income of the poorest pensioners more than other pensioners. Although all pensioners could have benefited from the additional Winter Fuel Payments, and those with sufficient contributions records could have benefited from the increases in the Basic State Pension, only pensioners poor enough to be entitled to means-tested income support (IS, HB or CTB) could have benefited from the much bigger increases made to these.
- Pensioners aged under 80 have seen bigger increases in their means-tested benefit entitlements than those aged 80 or over. This was due to the levelling-up of the age-related premia in the major means-tested benefits in April 2001. Before this, there were different (and increasingly generous) rates for pensioners aged 60-74, those aged 75-79 and those aged 80 or more (those on disability benefits, regardless of age were entitled to the highest rate). The distinction

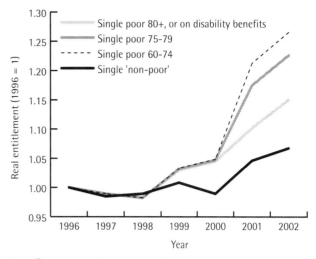

Figure 4.1: Increases in entitlements to benefits for single pensioners (April 1996–April 2002)

Notes: Figure shows entitlement to benefits that applied in April of that year. Real values were calculated using October values of all-items RPI index.

Source: Authors' calculations

between these premia was abolished in April 2001: all the rates were 'levelled up' to match the highest rate for pensioners aged 80 or over.

- Pensioners aged under 75 did not benefit from the free television licences, and the recent ad hoc help with Council Tax has had complicated rules relating entitlements to age.

Figure 4.1 summarises the percentage changes to benefit entitlements for different types of single pensioner between 1996/97 and 2002/03[2]. It plots the maximum weekly entitlement to state benefits for a single person, in real terms and indexed to 1 in 1996/97 for four groups of pensioners:

- 'non-poor': not entitled to IS/MIG
- 'poor and aged 60-74': entitled to IS/MIG and aged 60-74
- 'poor and aged 75-79': entitled to IS/MIG and aged 75-79
- 'poor and aged 80+': entitled to IS/MIG and aged 80 or over.

---

[2] It includes entitlement to IS/MIG and Basic State Pension (assuming complete contributions record), but does not include HB, CTB, Winter Fuel Payments, television licences, and ad hoc payments to help pay Council Tax bills. Figure 4.1 has adjusted nominal entitlements to benefit by the following October's RPI (retail price index) figure: this is not the same value that is used to uprate the benefits, and this is why Figure 4.1 shows some small year-on-year fluctuations in the real value of the entitlements.

Table 4.1: Changes in income, spending and entitlements to state benefits for four groups of single pensioners (1996/97–2002/03)

	% real change 1996/97–2002/03			£pw in 2002/03	
	Benefit entitlement	Income	Spending	Average income	Average spending
'Non-poor' (all over 59)	6.7	6.4	7.4	251	163
'Poor' (60–74)	26.5	33.4	20.5	134	105
'Poor' (75–79)	22.6	17.3	30.6	125	105
'Poor' (80+ or on disability benefits)	15.0	33.6	12.9	175	104

Notes: 'Non-poor' means not entitled to means-tested benefits under the tax and benefit systems of April 2002 (suitably adjusted for previous years). 'Poor' means entitled to means-tested benefits under the tax and benefit systems of April 1996 (suitably adjusted for subsequent years).

Source: Authors' calculations from FES and EFS from 1996/97-2002/03 combined with information in Figure 4.1.

The figure shows that entitlements stayed roughly the same in real terms for all groups for the first three years. From April 1999, increases to entitlements have been larger for the 'poor' than the 'non-poor'. From April 2001, younger 'poor' pensioners have done better than older 'poor' pensioners, because of the equalisation of the pensioner premia at the highest rate: by 2002/03; the poorest pensioners aged 60-74 had entitlements to IS around 27% higher in real terms than in 1996/97, compared to an increase of around 15% for those aged 80 or over; those not entitled to means-tested benefits saw a real increase of around 7% through rises in the Basic State Pension.

Increases in benefit entitlements and pensioner spending

So how do these increases in entitlements to state benefits relate to the changes to incomes and spending among pensioners?

Unfortunately, there is no household survey that tells us about changes in particular individual's income and spending[3], so, in

Table 4.1, we show the average percentage real terms changes in income and spending for four groups of single pensioners (as estimated in the FES/EFS). These groups were constructed by examining our estimates of their entitlement to means-tested benefits under the tax and benefit regimes of April 1996 and April 2002: we first assumed that the tax and benefit system in April 1996 (the least generous to pensioners between April 1996 and April 2002) was in force throughout the period 1996-2002 (suitably adjusted by RPI and ROSSI for the intervening years) and estimated entitlements to means-tested benefits, and then we did the same for the system in place in April 2002 (the most generous to pensioners between April 1996 and April 2002). The four groups are:

- 'non-poor pensioners': single pensioners who are not entitled to means-tested benefits under the April 2002 tax and benefit regime;
- 'poor and aged 60-74': entitled to means-tested benefits under the April 1996 tax and benefit regime and aged 60-74 (65-74 for men);
- 'poor and aged 75-79': entitled to a means-tested benefits under the April 1996 tax and benefit regime and aged 75-79;
- 'poor and aged 80+': entitled to means-tested benefits under the April 1996 tax and benefit regime and aged 80 or over or on disability benefits.

The aim is to construct one group of individuals that was not affected by the introduction of the MIG in April 1999 and its subsequent increases in generosity, and three

---

3   The British Household Panel Survey (BHPS) contains only very limited information on spending – for example, on food and utility bills – and only has information on expenditure bands rather than actual levels. Consumer panel data, such as that available from organisations like AC Nielsen and Taylor Nelson Sofres, typically contain only a very limited subset of expenditure on groceries such that they do not give a full picture of *total* household expenditure.

groups that were affected both by the introduction of the MIG and by the equalisation of the pensioner premia in the MIG in April 2001[4].

As well as showing the average percentage real terms changes in income and spending, Table 4.1 also shows the percentage change in benefit entitlements for the different groups of pensioners plotted in Figure 4.1 (see notes to the table for further details of definitions). At this stage, we have not taken into account any compositional changes in the different groups, which might also be driving the trends in income and spending.

Clearly, both pensioner incomes and spending have risen considerably during this period of rising entitlements. It is also apparent that poorer pensioners have increased both their incomes and their spending faster than richer pensioners. However, there does not, at this stage of our analysis (before we control for compositional differences in our samples), appear to be a clear and consistent relationship between the change in benefit entitlement for each of the groups, and the changes to average income and spending, especially for low-income pensioners of different ages.

Our statistical analysis, presented in full in the Appendix to this report, uses a linear regression to attempt to identify the impact on spending of the extra entitlement to benefits for pensioners. This allows us to control for any compositional differences in our samples, both over time and between the different groups of pensioners we have defined. We look at two different policy reforms:

- The introduction of the MIG in April 1999. Here we compare trends in spending between low-income ('poor') pensioners and ('non-poor') ones, focusing on whether the introduction of the MIG had a discernible differential impact on spending between non-poor and poor.
- The equalisation of the pensioner premia at the higher rate in April 2001. Here we

compare trends in spending between 'younger poor' pensioners and 'older poor' pensioners, assessing whether the reform has had a discernible differential impact on spending between these two groups.

If pensioners have spent more as their benefit entitlements have gone up, we would expect to see poorer pensioners' spending rising by more than richer pensioners', and younger poor pensioners' spending rising by more than older poor pensioners', assuming all other factors (except those that we can control for in our regressions) remain constant. The Appendix gives a more formal presentation of this evaluation strategy, known as the 'difference-in-differences' methodology, also used in Gregg et al (2005). Crucially, the method relies on the 'common trends' assumption: that in the absence of the reforms to pensioner benefits, the trends in spending among these groups would have been the same. This assumption cannot be tested.

We investigate the impact of the benefit reforms on four outcomes:

- disposable income (that is, income after tax and including all state benefits)
- non-housing expenditure
- basic non-housing expenditure, defined as fuel and food
- non-basic non-housing expenditure, defined as all spending except housing, food or fuel.

The key parameters of interest are shown in Table 4.2 (the full results are shown in the Appendix). This shows the additional percentage change in the outcome variables that we are attributing to the reforms: a positive value indicates that the outcome variable increased more rapidly after the reform for the group experiencing the bigger increase in benefit entitlements, which is what we would anticipate. Table 4.2 shows the difference in the logarithm of the outcome variables, which is approximately equal to the percentage change. Thus a figure of 0.1 suggests that the group experiencing the larger increase in benefit entitlements saw the outcome variable increase by around 10% more than those who did not see such an increase in entitlements.

---

[4] Some pensioners will be in none of the four groups: pensioners too rich to be entitled to means-tested benefits under the April 1996 tax and benefit system but who are entitled to means-tested benefits under the April 2002 tax and benefit system.

Table 4.2: Estimates of the impact of benefit reforms on various outcome variables for pensioners

	Specification 1	Specification 2	Specification 3	Specification 4
Impact of April 1999 introduction of Minimum Income Guarantee on 'poor' versus 'non-poor' pensioners				
Total income	0.114*** (0.024)	0.112*** (0.024)	0.100*** (0.022)	n/a
Non-housing expenditure	0.113*** (0.035)	0.096*** (0.034)	0.088*** (0.033)	0.086*** (0.033)
Expenditure on basics	0.039 (0.026)	0.030 (0.025)	0.024 (0.025)	0.024 (0.025)
Expenditure on non-basics	0.173*** (0.049)	0.149*** (0.047)	0.136*** (0.046)	0.136*** (0.046)
Impact of April 2001 equalisation of age-related premia to higher rate on 'young poor' versus 'old poor' pensioners				
Total income	0.015 (0.030)	0.016 (0.034)	0.012 (0.031)	n/a
Non-housing expenditure	0.079* (0.047)	0.097* (0.052)	0.092* (0.050)	0.099** (0.050)
Expenditure on basics	–0.006 (0.036)	–0.008 (0.041)	–0.011 (0.041)	–0.010 (0.041)
Expenditure on non-basics	0.142** (0.070)	0.184** (0.078)	0.178** (0.075)	0.189** (0.074)

Notes: See text for details. Standard errors in parenthesis. *** = significant at 1% level; ** = significant at 5% level; * = significant at 10% level.

We estimate four specifications of our basic model, each including other variables to help control for compositional changes over time in our sample. The four specifications are:

- A basic specification with no additional controls.
- A specification in which we control for region, having more than compulsory education, seasonality (through dummies for the quarter of the year), a time trend and a cubic in the year of birth of the head of household interacted with gender[5].
- A specification in which we also include dummies for disability and household tenure type, both of which may be endogenous to the receipt of means-tested benefits.
- For the expenditure regression, we also report a fourth specification, which includes a dummy for receipt of any income from investments. This may control for differences in income trends between our treatment and control groups, not related to the policy reform.

Finally, it should be noted that we restrict our estimation to pensioners who are not at the extreme top or bottom of the (pensioner)

income distribution – that is, the top or bottom 0.5% – and also remove pensioners for whom self-employment makes up a large share of their total income. Such households are highly unrepresentative of the pensioner population.

The results suggest that the introduction of the MIG in April 1999 has had the following effect on 'poor' pensioners (first panel in Table 4.2):

- a rise in their income of around 10 percentage points compared with that of richer pensioners;
- an increase in spending of a similar magnitude, little or none of which was on food and fuel: instead, poor pensioners increased their spending on non-basic items substantially compared with 'non-poor' pensioners.

The results suggest that the equalisation of the pensioner premia in April 2001 had the following effect on the 'younger poor' pensioners (lower panel in Table 4.2):

- a smaller than expected, and statistically insignificant, rise in income. This may be because incomes are not correctly reported among either the group subject to the reform ('younger poor' pensioners), or the comparison group ('older poor' pensioners). It may also be because of confounding trends in other elements of income. This latter explanation would mean that the 'common trends assumption' is violated;

[5] Note that in the EFS 2001/02, the age of the head of household is censored at 90; in 2002/03 it is censored at 80. Thus we cannot obtain the exact year of birth for some of our observations. To counter this we include in our specification a dummy for households with censored ages in each year.

- a rise in spending, of around 8 to 10%, with almost none of this extra spending being on basic goods: instead, spending on non-basic goods rose by around 15% and 20% more for the younger group than the older group.

These results can only serve as estimates of the impact of the changes to benefit entitlements on pensioners, because we can never know how much poor pensioners would have spent had the rises in benefit entitlements not taken place. Our estimates will be right, on average, if trends in spending among 'non-poor' pensioners are a good guide to trends in spending among poor pensioners (for the first set of estimates), and if trends in spending among older pensioners entitled to means-tested benefits are a good guide to trends in spending among younger pensioners entitled to means-tested benefits.

The common finding that any increases in expenditure were concentrated among 'non-basics' should not be interpreted as pensioners wasting their additional incomes on frivolous expenditure! Since non-basics are likely to be highly income elastic and basics highly income *in*elastic this result is exactly what we would anticipate. Pensioners will spend their income to meet their basic needs and then allocate additional expenditure to other items, many of which may indeed be essential for particular pensioners (clothing, travel costs and so on).

To check the robustness of our results, we ran a number of variants: our results were largely unchanged[6].

Conclusions

Although single pensioners on average have relatively high rates of income and spending poverty, we have shown that their income and spending have risen since 1999, as benefit entitlements have been increased.

Poorer pensioners have seen the biggest increases to their benefit entitlements, and have also seen the biggest increase in their spending. Our regression analysis, which attempts to control for other factors that might be driving these changes, suggests that benefit increases were the cause, and have particularly increased pensioner spending on non-basic items (that is, neither food nor fuel).

Poor pensioners aged under 80 have seen bigger benefit entitlement increases than those aged 80 or over since 2001. Although it appears that their spending, particularly on non-basics, has risen faster, a causal relationship between this and the equalisation of benefit rates is harder to find.

Overall, our findings suggest that the apparent paradox of static pensioner poverty measured with expenditure and falling pensioner poverty measured with income is not due to the fact that pensioners are saving all of their additional benefit entitlements.

There are various other explanations that might account for the difference in poverty trends among pensioners. One is that although the increases in income have been sufficient to pull some pensioners over the income poverty line, the commensurate increases in spending did not achieve the same result, either because part of the income was saved or because the pensioners most affected were further below the spending poverty line than the income poverty line in the first place. Alternatively, it could be that even if poorer pensioners have been spending higher incomes, expenditures among the rest of the (non-pensioner) population have simply been rising even faster, raising the poverty threshold still further.

---

[6]   In particular, we dropped the first year of our sample; we changed our definition of 'poor' to be just those households eligible to IS (rather than any means-tested benefit); we omitted pensioners less than five years older than the retirement age; we tried various definitions of 'income', varying the treatment of HB and CTB. Full results are available on request from the authors.

5

Conclusions and policy implications

This report has set out the reasons why household expenditure is an important complement to current household income for monitoring living standards and poverty. Although current incomes can be informative about an individual's short-term, or immediate, circumstances, expenditure is likely to be considerably more informative than current income about longer-term welfare. Although not without its measurement problems, those with the very lowest measured spending appear more likely to be experiencing genuine hardship, not simply due to measurement error, compared to those on the very lowest measured incomes.

The use of expenditure or consumption for monitoring living standards and poverty, although possibly unfamiliar in the British context, is widespread, particularly in developing countries where many individuals lack formal sources of income to fund their consumption, and where both self-employment and subsistence is widespread. Although it is in less common usage[1] in industrialised countries there is both a strong academic and empirical literature to support its use there too.

The case for assessing trends in expenditure poverty in Britain is strengthened by the fact that Britain has very good expenditure data. The EFS's combination of a two-week spending diary together with retrospective recall questions on more substantial or durable

items, provide an ideal combination for accurately measuring spending levels and patterns, but at the same time at least partially capturing more infrequent purchases. A clear drawback is the relatively small sample size of the EFS, especially compared to the FRS, which severely limits the amount of subgroup analysis possible. A useful addition would also be more information on the length of ownership and price paid for consumer durables already owned. This additional information would be particularly valuable in the light of the recent removal of durable ownership questions from the FRS, and would allow us to capture a much fuller picture of consumption levels than we are currently able to do.

One clear recommendation from this report, therefore, is that more attention is paid within the British poverty debate to trends in household expenditure. This could be achieved by the government adopting it as an indicator in *Opportunity for All*, or it could be for groups outside government to ensure this issue is regularly researched.

But there are also substantive lessons that we can learn from the findings of our report about both the effectiveness of the government's current anti-poverty policies, and the usefulness of the government's child poverty targets.

Our findings show that the relative success of the current government's policies for reducing current income poverty among families with children and pensioners needs to be set in its broader context. Although income poverty rates have come down significantly for both of these groups, the same cannot be said for expenditure poverty, which, in general, will

---

[1] This may reflect the fact that the discrepancy between expenditure and consumption is likely to be much greater in industrialised countries, where durable consumption is higher. Improved information about durable ownership in industrialised country surveys would help mitigate this problem.

capture better the longer-term differences between individuals than current income. The reasons for the different trends are not entirely clear, however, and understanding them better is an obvious area for future research. One obvious reason would be if people whose incomes had gone up through increases in benefits were not increasing their spending. Our investigation of changes in pensioner spending, however, found that at least some of the increases in means-tested benefits were being spent, and were being spent largely on non-essentials, consistent with a growing affluence among pensioners.

More generally, since spending inequality probably better reflects longer-term differences than income, our findings suggest that the government has had less success in reducing longer-term inequalities than it has in reducing short-term inequalities. This is consistent with very recent evidence on other aspects of longer-term inequality. For example, recent evidence produced by the Department for Education and Skills suggest that socioeconomic inequalities in school attainment have been rising (see DfES, 2005); similarly, inequalities in life expectancy and infant mortality have also continued to rise (see Department of Health, 2005). In all these cases, including the evidence we have shown in this report for household expenditure, the backdrop for widening inequality has been across-the-board improvements in (education, health or living) standards, but where the improvements for the majority outstrip those of the poorest.

What are the lessons for the government's future child poverty targets? A recurring theme throughout our report has been the strong likelihood that people recorded as being at the bottom of the income distribution either have their incomes measured incorrectly, or have very low incomes for very short periods of time, and the difficulty of distinguishing between the two with descriptive analysis such as that in this report. This has implications for the government's child poverty targets. Our evidence reinforces the government's view that it would be impossible for child poverty recorded using the current methodology ever to fall to 0. But it also suggests that the government's long-run aim of reducing child poverty to among the best in Europe by 2020

is likely to avoid moving into territory where incomes are a particularly poor guide to true living standards (either through mis-measurement or just transitorily very low income; in recent EFS data, this appears to affect mostly the bottom 2% of the income distribution). Although we are not suggesting in the light of our research that the government drops its income-based child poverty targets, and starts monitoring household expenditure instead, our research strongly suggests that anti-poverty policies would benefit from a closer and more regular scrutiny of spending inequalities and poverty.

References

Blow, L., Leicester, A. and Smith, Z. (2004) *Consumption Trends in the UK, 1975-99*, London: Institute for Fiscal Studies.

Blundell, R. and Preston, I. (1998) 'Consumption Inequality and Income Uncertainty', *The Quarterly Journal of Economics*, vol 113, no 2, May, pp 603-40.

Brewer, M., Goodman, A., Shaw, J. and Shephard, A. (2005) 'Poverty and Inequality in Britain: 2005', IFS Commentary 99 (www.ifs.org.uk/comms/comm99.pdf).

Brewer, M., Goodman, A., Myck, M., Shaw, J. and Shephard, A. (2004) 'Poverty and Inequality in Britain: 2004', IFS Commentary 96 (www.ifs.org.uk/comms/comm96.pdf).

Deeming, C. (2005) 'Minimum Income Standards: How Might Budget Standards Be Set for the UK?', *Journal of Social Policy*, vol 34, no 4, pp 619-36.

Department of Health (2005) 'Tackling Health Inequalities: Status Report on the Programme for Action', August (www.dh.gov.uk/assetRoot/04/11/76/98/04117698.pdf).

DfES (Department for Education and Skills) (2005) 'Has the Social Class Gap Narrowed in Primary Schools? A Background Note to Accompany the Talk by Rt Hon Ruth Kelly MP, Secretary of State for Education and Skills: Education and Social Progress', 26 July (www.dfes.gov.uk/rsgateway/DB/STA/t000597/index.shtml).

DWP (Department for Work and Pensions) (2003) *Measuring Child Poverty*, London: DWP.

DWP (2005) *Households Below Average Income 1994/95-2003/04*, Leeds: Corporate Document Services.

Goodman, A. and Oldfield, Z. (2004) *Permanent Differences? Income and Expenditure Inequality in the 1990s and 2000s*, Report Series No 66, London: IFS (www.ifs.org.uk/comms/r66.pdf).

Goodman, A., Johnson, P. and Webb, S. (1997) *Inequality in the UK*, Oxford: Oxford University Press.

Goodman, A., Myck, M. and Shephard, A. (2003) *Sharing in the Nation's Prosperity? Pensioner Poverty in Britain*, Commentary No 93, London: Institute for Fiscal Studies.

Gregg, P., Waldfogel, J. and Washbrook, E. (2005) 'That's the Way the Money Goes: Expenditure Patterns as Real Incomes Rise for the Poorest Families with Children', in J. Hills and K. Stewart (eds) *A More Equal Society? New Labour, Poverty, Inequality and Exclusion*, Bristol: The Policy Press.

Hills, J. and Stewart, K. (eds) (2005) *A More Equal Society? New Labour, Poverty, Inequality and Exclusion*, Bristol: The Policy Press.

Meyer, B. and Sullivan, J. (2003) 'Measuring the Well-Being of the Poor Using Income and Consumption', *Journal of Human Resources*, vol 38 (Supplement), pp 1180-220.

Meyer, B. and Sullivan, J. (2004) 'The Effects of Welfare and Tax Reform: The Material Well-Being of Single Mothers in the 1980s and 1990s', *Journal of Public Economics*, vol 88, nos 7-8, pp 1387-420.

Palmer, G., Carr, J. and Kenway, P. (2004) 'Monitoring Poverty and Social Exclusion 2004', New Policy Institute (www.npi.org.uk/reports/mpse%202004.pdf).

Parker, H. (ed) (1998) *Low Cost but Acceptable: A Minimum Income Standard for the UK: Families with Young Children*, Bristol: The Policy Press.

Parker, H. (ed) (2000) *Low Cost but Acceptable Incomes for Older People: A Minimum Income Standard for Households Aged 65-74 Years in the UK*, Bristol: The Policy Press.

Parker, H. (ed) (2002) *Modest but Adequate Budget for Pensioners April 2002 Prices*, London and York: Age Concern England and Family Budget Unit.

Slesnick, D. (1993) 'Gaining Ground: Poverty in the Post-war United States', *Journal of Political Economy*, vol 101, no 1, pp 1-38.

Appendix: Methodology for Chapter 4

In Chapter 4 it was explained that we hoped to learn about how pensioners responded to the increase in means-tested benefit entitlement by comparing the expenditure of those entitled to such benefits to expenditure patterns of other, otherwise comparable, pensioners. We made two comparisons – first, between poor pensioners under the age of 80, who were entitled to large increases in means-tested benefits as a result of the equalisation of pensioner premia, and poor pensioners over the age of 80 who did not benefit from this equalisation (we refer to this as the 'young/old' comparison). The second comparison was between all poor pensioners who received high increases in benefits and 'non-poor' pensioners who received a smaller benefit increase (this is the 'poor/non-poor' comparison). This Appendix details our methodology and results more thoroughly than was possible in Chapter 4.

Young/old comparison

Our sample consists of those pensioners eligible for any means-tested benefits (Housing Benefit, HB; Council Tax Benefit, CTB; or Income Support, IS) under the parameters of the 1996/97 benefits system, had there been no real change in benefits since that date. This helps ensure that the composition of our sample does not change simply due to the reform, since more people became entitled to benefits as a result of increased generosity between 1996/97 and 2002/03. This sample is split into two groups: those who benefited from the equalisation of the pensioner premia at the higher rate ('young cohort'), and those who did not ('old cohort'). The 'young cohort' of pensioners is defined as those who were

over state pension age in April 1996, but less than 80 at the time of the reform in April 2001 (that is, those men born between 1922 and 1931 or women born between 1922 and 1936). We define the 'old cohort' pensioners as those aged 80 or over in 2001 (that is, born in or before 1921), plus younger pensioners who were eligible to disability premia in IS: this is because, even before 2001, such pensioners were passported onto the highest pensioner premium (that is, that for people aged 80 or over) irrespective of age. The young cohort is referred to as the 'treatment group' and the older cohort the 'control group'. Note that we trim the top and bottom 0.3% of households from the income distribution in each year to prevent extreme values driving our results.

We define the period 1996/97 to 2000/01 as a 'pre-reform' period, during which entitlements to means-tested benefits for those over 60 rose equally regardless of age, and define the period 2001/02 to 2002/03 as a 'post-reform' period during which benefits for younger pensioners increased more rapidly (see Chapter 4, Figure 4.1). We use data from the 1996/97-2002/03 Family Expenditure Survey (FES)/Expenditure and Food Survey (EFS).

The definitions give us a sample of 3,056 pensioners who were or would have been entitled to any means-tested benefit under the 1996/97 system. This represents about 57% of all pensioners in the cohorts chosen for our analysis. While 63% of pensioners are eligible for any means-tested benefit in the 1996/97 data, this falls to 53% in 2002/03: this fall in eligibility is to be expected, because pensioners are getting richer over time. Our sample of 3,056 pensioners is split into 1,581 in the 'young cohort' (who received the relatively

Table A.1: Sample size in 'young/old' comparison groups

	Pre-reform	Post-reform	Total
Young cohort ('treatment group')	928	353	1,281
Old cohort ('control group')	1,385	390	1,775
Total	2,313	743	3,056

large increase in benefits) and 1,475 in the 'old cohort' (who received a smaller increase in benefits). After adjusting to take account of the fact that disabled pensioners also received the smaller increase, we are left with a treatment group of 1,281 pensioners (353 in the post-reform period) and a control group of 1,775 pensioners (390 in the post-reform period) (see Table A.1).

If instead of focusing on pensioners eligible for any means-tested benefit we instead focused on pensioners who were eligible for all three, we would instead obtain a sample of 1,802, or 34% of all pensioners. For our main analysis we focus on the group who are entitled to *any* means-tested benefit, but we also use the more restricted definition, of entitlement to *all* means-tested benefits, as an alternative specification. The former should pick up the effects of the policy change on a larger group, some of whom will not have taken up the benefits to which they were entitled (but may have been induced by the policy reforms to begin claiming means-tested benefits). The latter focuses on the effects of the policy reforms on a group who were already relatively likely to take up their benefit entitlements.

Non-poor/poor comparison

For this comparison, our 'treatment group' is now all pensioners entitled to any means-tested benefit under the (inflation-indexed) parameters of the 1996/97 benefits system. Again we focus on a cohort of pensioners who were of at least state pension age in all years of the sample, that is, men born in or before 1931 and women born in or before 1936. Our 'control group' is now pensioners who were *not* entitled to any means-tested benefit under the (inflation-indexed) parameters of the 2002/03 benefits system. This group can be thought

of as the 'never-entitled' since the 2002/03 system is the most generous of all the systems in our sample period – hence a pensioner not eligible for any means-tested benefit under this system would not be eligible under any other system since 1996/97 either. By contrast, our treatment group are those who are 'always-entitled' since the 1996/97 system is the least generous. This means there is a group excluded from this analysis, those pensioners who were not entitled to means-tested benefits under the 1996/97 system but who became newly entitled under the parameters of the 2002/03 system. For this group there is more ambiguity about the extent to which they benefited from the introduction of the Minimum Income Guarantee (MIG) in 1999.

For the non-poor/poor comparison, our post-reform period starts in 1999/2000, coinciding with the relatively large increases in entitlement for those eligible that began at that time (see Chapter 4, Figure 4.1). We have a total sample of 4,834 pensioners, of which around two thirds (by construction the same sample that formed both groups in the young/old comparison) are in the treatment group and one third the control group (see Table A.2).

Methodology

Our regression allows us to estimate what is known as a 'difference-in-differences' estimator, represented by the coefficient β_3 in the following regression:

$$\log Y = \beta_0 + \beta_1 T + \beta_2 POST + \beta_3 T * POST + \varepsilon$$

where Y is our variable of interest (whether income or expenditure), T is a dummy for the household being in the treatment group, $POST$ is a dummy for the post-reform period and an interaction term. The coefficient on the

Table A.2: Sample size in 'non-poor/poor' comparison groups

	Pre-reform	Post-reform	Total
Poor pensioners ('treatment group')	1,454	1,602	3,056
Non-poor pensioners ('control group')	737	1,041	1,778
Total	2,191	2,643	4,834

Table A.3: Difference-in-difference estimation results for log total income (young/old comparison)

	Specification 1		Specification 2		Specification 3	
$T*POST$ (diff-in-diff)	0.015	(0.030)	0.016	(0.034)	0.012	(0.031)
T	−0.170***	(0.015)	−0.321***	(0.020)	−0.044**	(0.021)
$POST$	0.120***	(0.021)	0.019	(0.031)	0.055**	(0.028)
Time trend	–		0.027***	(0.005)	0.022***	(0.005)
Year of birth	–		−0.154***	(0.037)	−0.063*	(0.033)
Year of birth^2	–		0.008***	(0.002)	0.004**	(0.002)
Year of birth^3	–		−0.000***	(0.000)	0.000**	(0.000)
Censored age (2001)	–		0.017	(0.109)	0.010	(0.098)
Censored age (2002)	–		−0.135***	(0.037)	−0.072**	(0.033)
Female	–		−0.397	(0.245)	−0.346	(0.221)
Year of birth*Female	–		0.080**	(0.040)	0.065*	(0.036)
Year of birth^2*Female	–		−0.004**	(0.002)	−0.004*	(0.002)
Year of birth^3*Female	–		0.000***	(0.000)	0.000**	(0.000)
Post-compulsory education	–		0.035**	(0.015)	0.069***	(0.013)
Disabled dummy	–		–		0.422***	(0.017)
Region dummies?	No		Yes		Yes	
Seasonal dummies?	No		Yes		Yes	
Tenure dummies?	No		No		Yes	
No. observations	3,056		3,056		3,056	
R^2	0.066		0.128		0.295	

Notes: Standard errors in parenthesis.

*** = significant at 1% level; ** = significant at 5% level; * = significant at 10% level.

interaction term, β_3, identifies the additional impact (on income or spending) of being in the young cohort after the reform, and it is our 'difference-in-differences' estimator. Since we regress logs of income and spending, the coefficient β_3 is approximately the extra percentage increase in income or spending enjoyed by the treatment group in the post-reform period relative to the pre-reform period, compared to the non-treated group. A positive value indicates that relative income or spending increased more rapidly after the reform for the treatment group than the control group, which is what we would anticipate. We also estimate further specifications of our basic model in which we include various other controls on the right-hand side, which may pick up compositional changes over time in our sample.

We assess the impact of the 2001 reform (for the young/old comparison) or the 1999 reform (for the non-poor/poor comparison) on income, expenditure, and expenditure on basic and non-basic items. We report several specifications for each, as detailed in Chapter 4:

- A basic specification with no additional controls.
- A specification in which we control for region, having more than compulsory education, seasonality (through dummies for the quarter of the year), a time trend and a cubic in the year of birth of the household interacted with gender[1].
- A specification in which we additionally include dummies for disability and household tenure type (both of these may not be exogenous to the receipt of benefits).
- For the expenditure regression, we also additionally report a fourth specification, which includes a dummy for receipt of any income from investments. This may control for differences in income trends between our treatment and control groups that is not related to the policy reform.

[1] Note that in the EFS 2001/02, the age of the head of household is censored at 90; in 2002/03 it is censored at 80. Thus we cannot obtain the exact year of birth for some of our observations. To counter this we include in our specification a dummy for households with censored ages in each year.

Table A.4: Difference-in-difference estimation results for log non-housing expenditure (young/old comparison)

	Specification 1		Specification 2		Specification 3		Specification 4	
*T*POST* (diff-in-diff)	0.079*	(0.047)	0.097*	(0.052)	0.092*	(0.050)	0.099**	(0.050)
T	0.016	(0.024)	−0.199***	(0.031)	−0.042	(0.035)	−0.046	(0.035)
POST	0.028	(0.032)	−0.008	(0.048)	0.019	(0.046)	0.011	(0.046)
Time trend	–		0.001	(0.008)	−0.006	0.007	−0.003	(0.008)
Year of birth	–		−0.119**	(0.057)	−0.074	(0.055)	−0.071	(0.054)
Year of birth^2	–		0.008**	(0.002)	0.005*	(0.003)	0.005*	(0.003)
Year of birth^3	–		−0.000**	(0.000)	−0.000*	(0.000)	−0.000*	(0.000)
Censored age (2001)	–		0.037	(0.169)	0.051	(0.163)	0.057	(0.160)
Censored age (2002)	–		−0.163***	(0.057)	−0.128**	(0.055)	−0.129**	(0.055)
Female	–		−0.279	(0.379)	−0.223	(0.366)	−0.173	(0.361)
Year of birth*Female	–		0.075	(0.062)	0.065	(0.060)	0.059	(0.059)
Year of birth^2*Female	–		−0.004	(0.003)	−0.004	(0.003)	−0.004	(0.003)
Year of birth^3*Female	–		0.000	(0.000)	0.000	(0.000)	0.000	(0.000)
Post-compulsory education	–		0.191***	(0.022)	0.148***	(0.022)	0.132***	(0.022)
Disabled dummy	–		–		0.242***	(0.028)	0.257***	(0.028)
Investment income dummy	–		–		–		0.182***	(0.020)
Region dummies?	No		Yes		Yes		Yes	
Seasonal dummies?	No		Yes		Yes		Yes	
Tenure dummies?	No		No		Yes		Yes	
No. observations	3,056		3,056		3,056		3,056	
R^2	0.004		0.072		0.135		0.162	

Notes: Standard errors in parenthesis.

*** = significant at 1% level; ** = significant at 5% level; * = significant at 10% level.

Table A.5: Difference-in-difference estimation results for log total income (non-poor/poor comparison)

	Specification 1		Specification 2		Specification 3	
*T*POST* (diff-in-diff)	0.114***	(0.024)	0.112***	(0.024)	0.100***	(0.022)
T	−0.647***	(0.018)	−0.593***	(0.019)	−0.712***	(0.019)
POST	−0.008	(0.019)	−0.109***	(0.028)	−0.116***	(0.026)
Time trend	–		0.032***	(0.006)	0.035***	(0.006)
Year of birth	–		−0.053	(0.033)	−0.023	(0.031)
Year of birth^2	–		0.002	(0.002)	0.001	(0.002)
Year of birth^3	–		−0.000	(0.000)	−0.000	(0.000)
Censored age (2001)	–		−0.117	(0.107)	−0.076	(0.099)
Censored age (2002)	–		−0.005	(0.029)	−0.040	(0.027)
Female	–		−0.594**	(0.235)	−0.490**	(0.218)
Year of birth*Female	–		0.083**	(0.038)	0.060*	(0.035)
Year of birth^2*Female	–		−0.004**	(0.002)	−0.003	(0.002)
Year of birth^3*Female	–		0.000*	(0.000)	0.000	(0.000)
Post-compulsory education	–		0.158***	(0.012)	0.177***	(0.012)
Disabled dummy	–		–		0.415***	(0.015)
Region dummies?	No		Yes		Yes	
Seasonal dummies?	No		Yes		Yes	
Tenure dummies?	No		No		Yes	
No. observations	4,834		4,834		4,834	
R^2	0.333		0.370		0.461	

Notes: Standard errors in parentheses.

*** = significant at 1% level; ** = significant at 5% level; * = significant at 10% level.

Table A.6: Difference-in-difference estimation results for log non-housing expenditure (non-poor/poor comparison)

	Specification 1		Specification 2		Specification 3		Specification 4	
*T*POST* (diff-in-diff)	0.113***	(0.035)	0.096***	(0.034)	0.086***	(0.033)	0.086***	(0.033)
T	−0.664***	(0.026)	−0.537***	(0.026)	−0.433***	(0.028)	−0.408***	(0.028)
POST	−0.055**	(0.028)	−0.058	(0.040)	−0.072*	(0.039)	−0.075*	(0.039)
Time trend	–		−0.003	(0.009)	−0.001	(0.009)	0.002	(0.009)
Year of birth	–		−0.045	(0.047)	−0.039	(0.046)	−0.035	(0.045)
Year of birth^2	–		0.003	(0.002)	0.003	(0.002)	0.003	(0.002)
Year of birth^3	–		−0.000	(0.000)	−0.000	(0.000)	−0.000	(0.000)
Censored age (2001)	–		−0.080	(0.152)	−0.034	(0.148)	−0.044	(0.146)
Censored age (2002)	–		−0.101**	(0.042)	−0.124***	(0.041)	−0.132***	(0.040)
Female	–		−0.296	(0.333)	−0.251	(0.323)	−0.193	(0.320)
Year of birth*Female	–		0.056	(0.053)	0.048	(0.052)	0.041	(0.051)
Year of birth^2*Female	–		−0.003	(0.003)	−0.003	(0.003)	−0.003	(0.003)
Year of birth^3*Female	–		0.000	(0.000)	0.000	(0.000)	0.000	(0.000)
Post-compulsory education	–		0.242***	(0.018)	0.209***	(0.017)	0.195***	(0.017)
Disabled dummy	–		–		0.234***	(0.023)	0.249***	(0.023)
Investment income dummy	–		–		–		0.171***	(0.018)
Region dummies?	No		Yes		Yes		Yes	
Seasonal dummies?	No		Yes		Yes		Yes	
Tenure dummies?	No		No		Yes		Yes	
No. observations	4,834		4,834		4,834		4,834	
R^2	0.202		0.263		0.304		0.317	

Notes: Standard errors in parenthesis.

*** = significant at 1% level; ** = significant at 5% level; * = significant at 10% level.

Our definition of income is total household income *including* any income from means-tested benefits and rent/Council Tax rebates: it is important to include rebates as income because the reform in April 2001 may have led some pensioner households to receive more HB or CTB even if their rent or Council Tax were unchanged, and this would free up income that could be spent[2]. We define expenditure as non-housing spending as usual. The coefficients are reported in full in Tables A.3 to A.6 for the two comparisons.

[2] Of concern, however, is the possibility that since rebates paid through CTB or HB depend on the Council Tax or rent bill faced by households, differential changes in the level of Council Tax or rent paid by treatment and control households will lead to biases in our estimator. Re-running our analysis excluding these rebates from income did not fundamentally change the findings.